# So You Write A Book

## HOW TO WRITE, SELF-PUBLISH* AND SELL YOUR OWN NON-FICTION BOOK

*OR ... A Viable Alternative To
Self-Publishing: The University Press

*For Susan*

*Good luck! 9/7/15*

## By Manny Luftglass

Gone Fishin' Enterprises
PO Box 556, Annandale, New Jersery 08801

# So You Want To Write A Book

## HOW TO WRITE, SELF-PUBLISH*
## AND SELL YOUR OWN NON-FICTION BOOK

*OR ... A Viable Alternative To Self-Publishing:
The University Press

© 2002 Emanuel Luftglass

Published by:

**Gone Fishin' Enterprises**
PO Box 566, Annandale, New Jersey 08801

www.gonefishinbooks.com

ISBN: 0-9650261-8-3
UPC: 7 9338095731-5

*Credits:*
Cartoons by Joe Perrone, photo on page 102 by Karen M. Peluso
and other photos by the author.

Trademarks and copyrights where applicable, shown on the appropriate pages.

*Design and Typography:* TeleSet, Inc., Hillsborough, New Jersey.

PRINTED IN THE UNITED STATES OF AMERICA

*To my wife Karen,*
*for all the obvious reasons*
*as well as those*
*that folks don't really know about,*
*thank you!*
*I love you, big time!*

# Acknowledgements

Two people more than others require acknowledgment. First: To Dr. Claudio Infantino of Rome, Italy, the New York trained Cardiologist who helped me recover from a heart attack on 8/26/01 in Italy and even accompanied me home — thank you! I call him Frank Buck, who, if you remember, was known for "Bring 'em back alive." Well, he sure did just that!

Second: To Dr. Paul DeRenzi of Mountain Lakes, NJ, another thank you! He was the Invasive Cardiologist who performed the angioplasty that cleared out my blocked artery, without which this book may not have been written.

# Table Of Contents

## About The Author

Manny Luftglass has written ten other books, of which eight are self-published and two published by a university press. He wrote three of the books with partners and the rest by himself. As a result, he will tell you what you need to know regarding writing, self-publishing, and selling your book, as well as describe a few interesting variations that he has personally experienced. You may find that his chapters on partnership and writing for a university press are quite helpful. As a retired insurance agent, his chapter regarding how to insure your own publishing company could be invaluable to you, as this subject is often overlooked in other books of this type. And he will carefully describe how to start your company.

Manny has written more than 1,500 articles and columns for a wide variety of magazines and newspapers since 1971. He had his own radio show for two years and appeared often on local television. Manny lectures in four eastern states.

Well-versed on a variety of topics, he is a former twice-elected Mayor of Somerville, NJ, and was the founder of the Somerville Environmental Commission. Manny served as a committeeman in Somerset, NJ, and on the Board of Adjustment in Clinton Township, NJ. He is a past President of the Independent Insurance Agents of Somerset County, NJ.

# Introduction

First of all, this book is intended to help you put a non-fiction book together. While many things you learn here might help you with a work that you try to create out of your own imagination, frankly, that would be merely a bonus. You see, the goal is to get you up and running with a product based solely in truth.

There are three basic subjects involved when you sit down to write your own non-fiction book. Simply put, they are:

1. **Writing the book!**
2. **Getting it published!**
3. **Figuring out how to get it sold!**

This simple illustration of what constitutes the make-up of a book could be called "The Nut Graf." In the January 2000 edition of *Writer's Digest,* David A. Fryxell tells his readers about this topic at length. In brief, he says, "Master the nut graf." This is the basic idea of an article or book and clearly, numbers 1, 2, and 3 make up the guts of what my book is all about, and is intended to get you to read on and learn how to perform each task.

Mr. Fryxell uses this to illustrate what writers of articles must do to get a reader to keep on reading. And while he tells us how important it is to get your attention immediately with a magazine article, it works just as well with a book.

He gives further examples of how to write and self-publish a book in an article he wrote for the same publication in its March 2001 edition. Just one idea alone is worth repeating, but to get the full gist of his thinking, do try to pick up a copy of that magazine. In that piece, Mr. Fryxell suggests that if you have particular expertise in a disease that has hit your own child, you might want to write about it so that other readers can share your knowledge.

So there's one more idea of what to write about, courtesy of this fine writer.

Continuing with thoughts from David Fryxell, in the September 2001 issue of *Writer's Digest,* he tells us to not worry about blank pages. His suggestion about your opening paragraph alone is well worth reading.

By the way, you will see reference to *Writer's Digest,* or *WD,* within this book many times. I view that publication as the most important magazine you can obtain in order to get as much additional information as you may find on the topic of writing a book. And while on the subject of useful sources, by all means, I hasten to also acknowledge how helpful Dan Poynter's book, "The Self-Publishing Manual" was to me. I call your attention to it several times within my book also. I talked to Mr. Poynter once and he was quite helpful to me.

CHAPTER ONE

# Writing The Book

Since you have apparently already decided that you want to write and self-publish your book, let's start thinking about the entire process in detail. You may have already researched the pros and cons of the so-called vanity or subsidy publishers. If not, check it out, but most writers will tell you that they have grave concerns about the reliability and costs of this method of production. Friends have told me that they paid a company to produce their book and, at best, got back very little in return.

So once you have established that you are going to take care of the entire matter by yourself, you have to establish a production game plan. After you decide what your subject matter is, you have to work out a schedule that fits your own particular needs and abilities.

## WHEN TO WRITE

This one is really more up to you than anything else. Only you can determine what time is best for you, and clearly, whether you are retired or not plays the biggest part in this decision.

Are you a person who needs eight hours of sleep each and every night, or can you make do with less? Are you a "night person," or a "day person?" Married or single? Parent with children at home? Of course, these factors play a huge role in helping you make the decision. But the bottom line is that time is needed, and you should pick those times that you feel are better suited to you for creativity. (Later on, when you are in the selling arena, you may find that other times are better.)

If you are creative at night, get to the computer after everyone else is tucked safely into bed, and start cranking! I wrote 90% of my first book between the hours of 11 p.m. and 2 a.m. because I simply couldn't sleep! My mind was racing so fast in connection with a business merger that writing the book during those otherwise insomniac hours was like medicine to me. And somehow or another, I didn't miss the sleep the following morning. Now that I am retired, I can pick my times to write with more ease — so you must be the one who makes the decision.

Weekends? Probably best, but don't eliminate your social life, and don't let your writing destroy your relationships with loved ones either.

In the November 2001 issue of *WD*, Raymond Obstfeld talks about finding the time to write. In brief, he suggests that, no matter who you are, you can find the time to write if you really want to do so. And is he right!

Steven James wrote a great piece for *WD* in their February 2000 issue, heading it "Jump-Start Your Brain." Tying directly into the topic of when to create, he offers a humorous illustration of what some writers feel they are facing when their brain gets all locked up. Mr. James provides lots of ideas about how to get your typing fingers all cranked up and running in that article. It's worth reading!

As you start poring through my book, be encouraged rather than discouraged, please. Just realize that half of your friends also want to write a book about something, but don't have a clue how to do it. Chances are that well over 50% of people who are 50 years of age have one or two stories they want to tell but don't know where to begin. And since you have started the process, you have a giant leg up on them.

When you kick your idea into gear, think about some words of wisdom I found in the January 2000 edition of *WD*, written by Greg Daugherty. He suggests targeting Baby Boomers as your primary book buyers. Daugherty says that four million Americans are turning 50 each year, and that doesn't even count the folks in other countries who may be possible buyers of your book as well. Among the topics he suggests for your book would be health, retirement advice, travel, humor, and a variety of other interesting ideas. He covers a wide variety of topics, but make note that if you tell people about any of these items as it applies to folks in their general age group, you will be hitting the main book buyers.

Mr. Daugherty, quoting from The NPD Group, tells us that readers who were either under the age of 25, or between 25 and 29, spent an average amount of 24 minutes reading daily between the years 1992-1998. But those in the 55-64 age range much more than doubled that time reading. They put in 53 minutes daily!

So write to a target audience of folks who have more time to read about things that you expect will be of interest to them, to have a better shot at success.

## ERRORS

Boy, this one can kill you! No matter what, your book will contain quite a few mistakes. Some may involve the basic content itself (hopefully not many), but most will be spelling or number errors. And of course, a few may just be close to unavoidable. When I wrote an article for *Nick Jr.* magazine, a "Fact-Checker" contacted me with many questions to ascertain accuracy. And while she asked some fine questions, it helped me to actually discover a few problems in what I had written, without her talking about the specific matters!

Looking for errors and finding them are two different subjects, but no matter what you write about, you really want

CHOICES

to tell the true story without creating confusion with wrong material.

When you write your book, first seek another expert on the topic and speak to her or him in advance, asking for a review of your material. The more time your reviewer spends, the better, and you may even want to offer financial compensation for such service.

Three sets of eyes are even better than two. Ask someone to look at what you consider the "finished" book for detail mistakes. And get another person to look into specific facts that you talk about, to make sure they are correct. While you are at it, how about someone to examine two key error areas that your spell checker cannot find fault with — numbers and proper names?

Whenever you write a number, check it out. You may have intended to write 22 and instead typed in 221. Needless to say, this will not come up as an error in your spell check. While typing this very book, I typed the name of one of the experts whose information I quoted from incorrectly! That would have been incredibly embarrassing had I not found the problem.

Going back to my favorite source, *WD*, in their January, 2000 issue, Britta Waller wrote, in part, herself quoting from another source: "The journalism adage," 'If your mother tells you she loves you, check it out,' The message being, no matter what, make sure of what you write.

In that same article, Ms. Waller offers a list of "Red Flags," giving examples of the subjects that most often have inaccuracies. Among the hot spots were proper nouns, math, and tall tales. Correctly stated, she feels that these are places that fact-checkers really need to concentrate their attention. After all, your spell check or grammar program won't verify arithmetic!

And in another article, this time in the September 2001 issue, written by Dean M. Shapiro, he gave more examples of how a spell check alone doesn't get it all done. Besides checking spelling and grammar via your word processor, he offers a lesson to learn, warning readers to hire a professional editor if they have any doubt.

Let me extend that thought a bit. "Editors" can be quite expensive, but most publications have "fact-checkers" who can also serve in the capacity of helping with other technical glitches that you fear may be possible. If you are already writing a column somewhere, ask your editor for permission to talk to who she/he uses to assist with fact checking for that publication. And if you are not in print somewhere already, call your local hometown newspaper and try to get an editor on the phone. Ask that editor if you can hire someone to fact check your book for you via the moonlight route. Don't ever do these things if you suspect that you are asking someone to work for you while on the payroll of another, though!

## WRITING FOR YOUR COMPANY

It is quite possible that you work for a major corporation that might want to commission you to write a book about itself. The book could be about its history, perhaps a work that they might use to assist in sales, or a manual to give out to new employees. In this case, you might still want to get the book printed yourself but chances are great that your employer will want to take care of the whole venture. In any case though, if you are doing the job for your company, selling it will be a major burden that you won't have to be concerned about.

If you consider yourself a writer, and bought this book (or took it out at your local library) with the intent of determining how to write a book about your hobby and instead was inspired to try to write one about your employer, that's great!

Therefore, if you have access to corporate management and know that a great story exists but was never written about the company, or that the employee manual is so terribly out of date (or was never written), go for it! Get to corporate management with the idea and be persistent. If you are well thought of, you might just be able to get authorization from the boss to write the story.

If you do write a book about your corporation, it will make book numbers two and three even easier to produce. And if your subsequent books are about anything else at all, you still will be able to call yourself a "published author" and that will make selling #2 lots easier indeed, trust me!

## WHAT GOES INSIDE?

Your designer/typesetter will be invaluable to you to make that first page grab the eyes of your reader. Give them something to look forward to that you know will appeal to readers of your kind of book, and you have better than a 50% chance that they will buy it!

Pick up any book at all, perhaps this one, and look at how

it lays out. Except for the covers, which will be discussed several times as you read on, each book should have the following:

■ **Title.** And don't take this one lightly at all! We all know that some readers do feel that they can "tell a book by its cover." We will talk about the cover appearance later, but of extreme importance to the success of your book is what you call it! So pick your title very carefully, please.

Again, referring to *WD*, I came across an article written by Christina Hamlett in the June 2001 issue. She suggests that a writer should make their title quite brief but provocative.

Here's one very specific reason for this idea. Just to illustrate, let's talk about the wholesaler who will ultimately offer your book to stores for sale. In their catalogs, they may show the whole book title, but via the internet, they may not. I discovered that my book titles were too long and were not fully revealed in listings by one wholesaler.

For example, I wrote about the best fishing waters in Connecticut and Pennsylvania and they left the states out. The titles were shown as merely "Gone Fishin'...The 50 Best Waters in __ . and "Gone Fishin', the 75 Best Waters in __ . So stores in Connecticut and Pennsylvania that have separate "local interest" sections had no reason to order because these book titles were too long. They couldn't identify that the books were about their states as a result of my title being longer than the wholesaler had room for in their listing.

Hopefully, my title "So You Want To Write A Book" fit everyone's screens. Of course, extending a title or adding a sub-title is very important and can help you immensely. Your title really needs to tell people what the book is all about. And except in rare cases, that title may not even be yours alone to use. My friend Ron Bern wrote a book that he called "The Legacy" and then later discovered that at least a half-dozen other books had first been written with that very same title. Actually, I would rather have preferred to use the title that

Dan Poynter used, "The Self-Publishing Manual," but didn't want to copy it, opting instead to use my own. I hope the sub-title, "How To Write, Self-Publish, And Sell A Non-Fiction Book," helps to get readers to know what the book is about.

■ **Dedication.** To your spouse? Maybe. This is your page, set aside to pay tribute to someone very special. Use it wisely and sincerely.

■ **Acknowledgements.** You can fill up a page or two just involving folks or places or clubs who have helped you create your work of art. A scholar to whom you owe a debt of gratitude? Certainly, if such an IOU exists, but just understand one thing — no one cares! Honestly, other than a handful of readers, hardly anyone will even read the acknowledgements page. In this book, since I suspect that I might not otherwise have been around to write it, there were two such people I just had to acknowledge. But, chances are that you didn't read that page, right? So write your acknowledgements page, for sure, but don't get too preoccupied with it.

■ **Copyright page.** This page lists the information about the physical book itself. The date of publication or previous publications and the revisions, the person(s) who has rights to this material, the ISBN, Library of Congress and other numbers of identification, the publisher and how to reach them, the designer, illustrator or photographer, along with the origin of printing. This page typically carries a disclaimer, reserving all rights to the author or publisher. It is interesting to note that once you write a book, and place that little copy-right symbol on your copyright page, it is your property — for life, plus 70 years.

■ **Table of Contents.** Extremely important! While some people may buy your book because they heard about it and publicity pre-sold it for you, many buyers pick it up by chance.

We will get into ways to attract "by chance" buyers later on, but if someone stumbles onto the book, one of the first things they will look at is the Table of Contents! So make sure you have one in your book and that it lists each chapter's subject matter.

Early on, whatever your topic, you should put down a list of subjects that need to be separately written about. You might only want five or six chapters, but a chapter list is extremely important to the book, and it will help you sell it to people whose eyes have been caught that way.

■ **Introduction.** This could be a place for you to tell your own story in brief. Some writers tell why they wrote the book. Others will go into their own personal history (and not many readers will care). Of most importance though, is to actually lay out what the book is all about in the introduction.

■ **Foreword.** This could be especially meaningful if some-one who is well-known in your subject matter agrees to write it for you. Giving space to a well-known expert on your topic may be viewed by that person as a compliment, but truthfully, you will be a benefactor as well. A stranger who knows more than you might be someone to quote within the book, but if a well-known person offers help, putting that material in as a foreword may be quite beneficial to you. If the person is extremely popular, you might even want to place her/his name on the front cover of your book and use that informa-tion in your sales approach later on.

■ **Index.** If you are writing about birds, you might get stuck listing robins in your index on 30 or 40 pages, so be careful with what you put in the index. Names of people? Yes, certainly, tell your readers where to find data about those folks. Cities or states? Yes, of course. You really need to use common sense when you put your index together or else it will be more clutter than useful. But clearly, an index is important and often quite helpful to your readers. In my chapter about university presses, I list them in alphabetical order by state, and then again in alphabetical order within states that have multiple university presses. Therefore, it really is foolish to again list all of these schools in the index, and as a result, I omitted them.

■ **Glossary** and **Appendix.** These are separate groupings that I found in Dan Poynter's book, but you may find no need to put these into the back of your book. Your subject matter will determine whether or not you want to go into much more than just an index after you are finished with the book.

■ **Bibliography** — you may want to add this. A bibliography is a listing of other books, articles or materials that you consulted when writing your book. Where you got some of your information might be helpful to readers if they want to do further research on their own.

■ **Colophon.** Not many books contain this page since it is mainly of interest to other designers or book collectors. Here you will find design statistics such as typestyles and layout software. It can be very detailed, or very simple, listing interesting facts about the physical book itself, such as specialty papers (if used) and the number of actual books printed. This page can add elegance to your book and define it as a "limited edition," suggesting immediate collectability.

■ **Order Form.** If you have the extra pages, why not include a convenient order form? After all, you're main purpose here is to sell books, and when they buy direct from you — the higher the profit. This is a great way to stir an interest in other books you may publish. Be sure to include a check box asking them if they want to be added to your mailing list.

■ **Note(s) Pages**. Add this/these pages as a convenience

to your readers. This is where they can make their own notes for future use.

## PREPARING TO WRITE A BOOK

Let's walk through this process in greater detail.

Let's say that you were a journalism major in college, but maybe 10-20 years ago. You may have studied writing along with other subjects, but chances are that you really need some more knowledge about writing before starting to write your first book.

If you have a column in a newspaper, or for that matter, any creative writing experience at all in your workday routine, it will help. But if you intend to put out the very best work you can, and get someone to buy it too, it may be time to sign up for additional courses.

Just as an example, I looked at the course offerings in the Spring, 2002 booklet put out by my local polytechnic institute. Remember, I live way out in the boondocks and it is quite possible that this school teaches more about cow milking and corn growing than writing, okay?

The particular itinerary shows separate courses on travel writing, life stories, and technical writing. And these three courses are far from all that are available in my county, because it also offers plenty of night classes.

Moving a bit closer to city streets, but still a school that is far from the hustle and bustle of a big town, I called a nearby community college about its Adult Education Class offerings and was told about the following classes: "Communication Through Effective Writing," and "Business Writing."

And in their English Department, they offer still three more separate classes about how to write. In fact, years ago, I took a class at that school in sports writing! In addition, the college itself offers regular ongoing writing classes to its full time students.

So, even if you think you know all you need to know about

The dreaded "writer's block"

how to write a book, if you only know it in principle and would like to learn still more before you get started, sign up for a class or two. Honestly, you can even do both. Get your book cranked up and underway all at the same time as you start your classes. If you tell your teacher about your project, she/he may be able to help you as well.

One key thing that all instructors try to preach:

*Get them listening — right away!*

You want to capture your reader's attention instantly, so when you begin your book, don't put them to sleep! Start it out with something really interesting about its topic. When I took my class in sports writing, I remember clearly that the teacher told us to use the first paragraph well to "hook" your reader. Tell them something about the book, or in one way or another, get their attention.

It is far more important to begin with a bang when you are writing an article for a magazine, but with books too, give your reader something to look forward to right at the start.

If you are writing about birds in your state, don't begin by saying that there are lots of sparrows in it. Instead, tell them about the yellow-bellied sapsucker you once saw and at what time and where it was. Clearly, bird-watchers will be more inclined to read your book if you wham them right smack in the eye with something of great interest from the very get-go!

Putting your thoughts down on paper is not a difficult task, but how to organize them with proper continuity is very challenging, and requires advance thinking. And, I trust, you are computer literate and understand what that gray box in front of you is all about before you get into the driver's chair and start pounding your words out.

There will be times that you just cannot think at all. Creating words? Heck, you may not even be able to remember how to spell cat or dog! Don't worry about this. Just go out and do something else. Go shopping, maybe visit your library to read up on your subject matter, anything else but get concerned that your mind has shut down. It happens to every one of us, often, honest!

By the way, here's something I learned from reading "The Self-Publishing Manual" by Dan Poynter, a book that I will refer to from time to time in this book — and it's so simple that I am shocked that so few do what he suggests — start with page #1! And what does that mean?

Simply, any page inside the front cover should be counted as a page, not as a Roman numeral. Until now, in all of my self-published books, my dedication, foreword, all rights reserved, etc., pages had Roman numerals instead of numbers on them. Poynter feels and I certainly agree that this is a mistake. When a buyer looks at a book, they see content, appearance, cost, and number of pages.

Somehow, many equate cost with the number of pages and even if your book was printed based on it having 128 pages, unless you number them, the buyer may think otherwise. For example, my book, "Gone Fishin' In Lake Hopatcong" had 12 pages that preceded the first page of the first chapter. Why? Because I didn't think I had an alternate until I read Poynter's book. And potential buyers of my Hopatcong book thought that it had fewer pages then it actually had. So, a word to the wise, count each and every page that has copy on it as a page, okay?

Another idea that I got from Mr. Poynter is to use the last few pages of your book as order forms. Remember, printers print 16 pages on a large sheet of paper. These 16 pages are then folded, trimmed, and collated. In a perfect bound book, each group of 16 pages is placed one on top of each other and bound. So your finished book will always have a multiple of 16 pages (example: 160 pages equals 10 16's). You can have $10\frac{1}{2}$ 16's, or 168 pages but the price will be the same as 11 16's or 176 pages... so go for the full multiple of 16.

Therefore, if you are done with the book at 156 pages and have to pay for 160, why not use the four extra pages you paid for as order forms? Let the reader of your book clip a page at the end out to use for ordering more copies of the book — to give as presents, etc.

Blank pages cost you just about the same thing as printed ones — you are paying for paper, mainly! As an alternative, head such otherwise blank pages as "NOTES." If you have written a book that lends itself to such an idea, then when you are all done, let your reader scribble notes in the back of the book on "NOTES" pages. Instead of footnotes that they write on printed pages, they can write what they want on the blank note pages that you provided for them, and they will appreciate it!

## REGIONAL VERSUS UNIVERSAL APPEAL

I trust that you have already made the decision regarding whether to self-publish or not. Now let's try to figure out if you want to go for a grand-slam home run for your first time up at the plate or a simple bases-loaded single.

We all seek a spectacular success the first time out of the box. The problem here is whether to go with a regional book, country or worldwide. If you write a book that is about a universally popular subject, one that you truly feel you know enough about to gain the interest of readers everywhere, then by all means, go for it, please. Of course, you also have to do research on the topic to expand your book into the best product you can put out. Even if you have been involved your entire lifetime with the subject matter, you cannot imagine how much more you can learn through research. Therefore, don't be so bold as to think that you can write your book without help.

What you must know though is that for every non-fiction book that is not based on regional material, there are tons of them that simply do not sell. Local interest books usually do better.

If you have countless dollars to advertise your book with, and are imaginative and creative enough to generate sales one at a time, then you may not need to find the chain buyers who make decisions about books that they will put into all of their stores.

This also involves libraries and wholesalers; in fact, any one who looks at your book may either like or dislike it. Once again, if it is widely accepted, a book that is not regional in scope can make a bundle of money. Restricting a book to a specific area dramatically reduces your prospective sale totals. The big problem though, by far, is to find someone to buy it. Someone at home, yes, but moreover, the folks at the largest retail stores — Borders, Barnes & Noble®, Walden. If they don't buy it, you just don't sell it in great bulk unless you generate enormous sales through individual purchases.

My own feeling is that it is far easier to sell a regional book because the market for them is really huge. Every bookstore of any size has a section that is devoted to its own area. It could be called "Local Interest," or "Regional," or something like that. Again, public and school libraries also have separate sections for books that are about the area their patrons/ students live in.

If your subject is flea markets, then write about those that are in your state. Sure, tell them how to start one, and add all the information you know and have learned, but readers are most interested in buying non-fiction books that touch home, literally! That home could be somewhere else too. If you are writing to folks who live in a cold climate, try adding a chapter or two on the subject matter about what is available in, for example, Florida!

A flea market junkie who lives in Maine may not have many outdoor places to take their bag of coins to up home in January but if they are traveling south, they surely will want to know about the places that they can hit in, say, Boynton Beach, Florida.

My book, "Gone Fishin' For Carp," discusses fishing for such a species everywhere. It wouldn't have made sense to write a book about going after this fish in a single state or area, unless an enormous number of anglers had interest. On the other hand, a book about fishing for carp in Great Britain, where "Carpers" abound in huge number, wouldn't be a bad idea at all. There have been quite a few books specifically written about fishing for trout in a single state, and because trout are a more popular target, that concept has worked well.

So after you have chosen your subject, decide if you want to write about it in your own home state or region, where you probably have significant information (in your head, accessible through your library, and through folks you know). To repeat, your opportunity to achieve success is much greater if you go local. (See the chapter on university presses for more material on this matter.)

## IT'S SO MUCH EASIER NOW!

Let's take that horrible, awful killer day — the one where you are so mentally blocked up that you feel that finishing your book is an impossible task. That's the day to realize how easy it has all become now. Like we already said, forget about the block and think how much worse it was years ago. Just imagine the olden days when a writer would actually write! Blank pages, loose leaf pads, or who knows what else was put into play and such compilations of paper actually wound up with it all, somehow or another, fitting into a book format one day. Later on, most writers changed over to typing their books on the old black manual typewriter, then switching over to electric when they came out. But the advent of the computer changed all that and I trust you will be writing your book on one.

Using a computer allows an author to make changes with relative ease, and to review and re-review as often as need be. On the other hand though, you had better learn how to "save" your words in several ways because disaster lies ahead of you in the form of a !*&CRASH^%!

## BACK IT UP!

Since computers are known to crash and burn from time to time, you need to prepare for the worst, knowing that it may take years for the problem to occur. Just having planned for such an occasion can give you the comfort level needed to not worry in advance.

Simply, back it up is what you must remember! Back up what you write at least daily, and if you really are in the chair, banging page after page out, do it at least every hour!

Back up your words in several ways. First, "save" the book, but make sure to have a little sticky on your computer telling you what you "saved" it as, especially if your machine holds a lot of saved files.

If you are very productive, working fast and getting whole

chapters done in a single day, then you might want to put the book on a separate disk every day. If you get 5-10 pages finished each day, at least stick it all on a disk a couple of times a week. If you are doing well and the devil "writer's block" has not knocked you to your knees, make sure to print out everything not less than once a week with the date and page numbers on each page.

Printing the book as it exists each week will be most useful to you too. Your spell check, no matter how good, will not pick up many errors. Physically reading what has been printed will reveal many otherwise missed errors.

Of course, "saving" the book in your computer will be useless if the machine crashes, but at least most problems can be solved with backups, other than a total crash. A power failure, electrical storm, etc., could stop you mid-work, and remove everything you typed that day, but if you saved what was done until yesterday, at least all of that work will probably be held and available.

Thinking like an old insurance agent (which, I guess, I am), let's continue on this pessimistic tone, and be ready for almost everything. Assume you saved the book in your computer, and copied what you had on a disk, and also printed everything done so far on paper. Are you ready for anything now? Well, no! What if you have a fire?

You need to keep duplicates of nearly everything. No, not on two computers in two premises — that's not practical. But if you put the book as it exists on a disk, put that disk somewhere else. Keep it in your car (as long as it's not summer) or better yet, if you work somewhere else, update it daily and take a copy of the disk back and forth each day to your office, store, shop, etc., and take the printed copy with you too. In any case, you have a back up of a back up and are prepared and ready for just about everything.

I learned the hard way, and therefore I am warning you. You see, until a few years ago, I never had saved a book on a disk! I only saved it in the computer once in a blue moon. In addition, I had only printed it periodically, with no rhyme or reason beyond that. And my gray box not only crashed, it darn near blew up! Don't ask me what took place, but suffice it to say that the memory went to Alzheimer's! Nothing, but nothing, remained within the machine, and lots of help went to naught. My son Henry is a computer genius but he was no better than illiterate regarding how to get anything back. At his suggestion, I took the machine to the best "fixit" shop around, and left it for a few days, but the resident computer doctor deemed that the patient was dead!

A book that I was writing was 90% done, and all that I had left of it was approximately 60%, printed on paper. It took me quite a while to remember and retype the 40% that was not on paper, and longer yet to finish the book completely on the new computer that I bought.

The 60% that was saved on paper was typed into a computer by an expert typist, but she made several mistakes when copying it onto a disk, which involved non-spell check words, and I had to read and re-read it all and correct it myself.

So, a book that was 90% done in my computer was held back from finishing by my own failure to save it properly.

And did I mention that I had hundreds of stories in the computer, and just after it crashed I was offered the opportunity to resell them for thousands of dollars?

I hope that you have learned from my telling you about this foolish error of mine!!

## PUTTING IT ALL TOGETHER

It doesn't much matter how fine a piece you put out, unless you can find a team of players who can make the book look good, you don't stand a chance!

## DESIGN/TYPESETTING

Your designer/typesetter can help you design the entire book, up to and even including the cover itself. Remember, without an attractive cover, you stand little chance at selling big numbers of your creation!

So, without further ado, here are a few places to outreach to. Note that many professionals specialize in the design of covers. Some also take care of your typesetting needs, and still others will help you market your book. It really is up to you regarding what you feel your needs are. If you think that you can handle the marketing yourself, or better yet, have located a specialist in that field, then try to find someone who will take your words and pictures and create magic with them. Again, if you know how to set type well, perhaps you might only want a cover designer. Frankly, I would rather get someone who does both!

Listed herewith in alphabetical order are five small companies that perform the two critically important skills that are needed to help you present your work well. I obtained four of the names from Dan Poynter's book, and the fifth is the woman who has done what was needed for me for my nine self-published books.

I spoke directly to each of the four other experts to make sure that they can do for you what I suggest, and each can indeed do that. If you would like a longer list of such people, try to check out Dan's book from your library, or buy a copy. The five companies are:

■ **Arrow Graphics, Inc.** (Ms. Alvart Badalian) based in Massachusetts, her telephone number is 617-926-8585 and fax number is 617-926-0982.

■ **Robert Howard Graphic Design** (Mr. Robert Howard) works in Colorado, and can be reached at 970-225-0083 and he also uses that number for faxes.

■ **Knockout Design** (Ms. Peri Poloni) is based in California, telephone number- 530-676-2744 — fax # 530-676-2741.

■ **Phelps & Associates, LLC** — is headed by Janice Phelps in Ohio. Her phone # is 740-689-2950 and fax 740-689-2951.

■ **TeleSet, Inc.** (Stephanie Ward) is in New Jersey, and her phone number is 908-359-1514 (fax is 908-359-0137).

In my old line of work we used to tell our clients that "I am as near as your telephone" and to some extent, that is really true. However, if you find someone who can help you with your needs who you can actually visit with in person, you really might want to go that way. That's why I selected companies that are not all situated in one area. Yes, with the internet being what it is, you can work with people without ever meeting them, but if the price is right and you can drive there, to your printer or your designer/typesetter, agent, etc., by all means, do it!

I sought out some pearls of wisdom from Stephanie Ward of TeleSet who produced all of my self-published books. This was done so that you could get some basic thoughts of what a designer/typesetter needs to produce a book for you. I urge you to consult more than one expert before you hire anyone, of course. I print her ideas because she has been the only one that I have needed to use for production to date.

## ADVICE FROM A DESIGNER/TYPESETTER

"Hopefully, you will heed Manny's fine words of wisdom and invest in a computer and a printer if you are seriously considering self-publishing a book. You don't need a top-of-the-line system, just one that offers a basic word processing program. I would suggest the software program called "Word®" from Microsoft. Not only is it powerful, it is easy to use and has many helpful features such as spell-check, grammar-check, and thesaurus help. It also comes with database capabilities to help you maintain a mailing list when it comes time to make those sales.

As for the printer, any color inkjet printer will do. Try to choose a popular brand, such as Hewlett-Packard® (HP), Canon® or Lexmark® to take advantage of their great warranties. You needn't spend more than $100 on these.

It's important to seek the services of a professional designer/typesetter in the early stages of your writing. This should be done after your first draft, and before final editing. Don't wait until your book is complete and rush into choosing someone who really can't accomplish what you want. Some professionals simply typeset, while others can walk you through the entire process, from typing your first word to delivery of your books, offering advice along the way that can make your life easier.

Always ask to see a portfolio. Look for someone who has completed a number of books — which you like — that you would buy. Commercial printing and book printing are very different, each requiring specific knowledge. You'll need a designer who has experience managing large amounts of information, and the expertise to supply your printer with a clean, error-free disk for book production.

Advances in printing technology have soared in recent years. Most cost-effective book printers use a process called "direct-to-plate." This means you hand them a disk, and the type and images are downloaded directly to the plate. The plate is then put on the press. This process has streamlined the printer's world by eliminating the need for labor-intensive tasks, which is great for you because it saves money and turnaround time. The "direct-to-plate" method does require that the designer be extremely computer literate — up-to-date in their hardware, software, and skill. Always ask what software they use and be sure it is professional quality typesetting/layout software. QuarkXpress® and Adobe

PageMaker® are two good examples. If the printer can't use the disk, you can't get a book.

Always get an estimate. Before you meet with a prospective designer/typesetter, take a trip to your local bookstore or library. Get a few books that you really like the look and feel of. Bring these along and discuss how you feel about your book. This will make it easier for the designer to nail down a realistic price. The text (inside) pages are usually priced-per-page, based on size and layout complexity. The text pages can run from as little as $10 per page to as much as $40 per page. Other costs such as design, scans of supplied art and photographs, illustration, or professional photography, if necessary, should all be priced separately.

Be sure that the estimate includes a realistic page count. Many factors affect the number of pages your book will ultimately contain, such as typestyle/type size, number of photographs/illustrations, and chapter beginnings/endings. Still, without a realistic page count, you won't be able to get printer estimates, you won't know how much to charge, and you won't know if you'll be able to make a profit.

Be specific with your designer. Let them know what you expect. Tell them how many pages would be comfortable and affordable for you. If you've envisioned a 200-page paperback, tell them so. A good designer can tell you what is possible and offer alternatives to help keep within your budget.

Submit a clean disk and a clean manuscript to your designer/typesetter. The more work you do, the less you will have to pay for. Editing is very time-consuming and expensive, and unless you have included this cost in your budget, brush up on your punctuation and grammar. After you have completed your book, ask some friends to give it a read. You'll be amazed at what they'll find. It's nearly impossible for you, as the author, to catch silly mistakes — you're just too close to the words. The book you write is a direct reflection on you, and you'll want it to be as correct as possible, in your subject matter, and in your writing style. When in doubt, pick up *The Chicago Manual Of Style*. This book contains everything you need to know about writing style.

Once you have submitted the disk and manuscript and typesetting has begun, be aware that changes made at this point are considered "author's additions" or AA's. You will be billed for the time it takes the designer/typesetter to makes your changes. This can add up, so try to avoid this step. However, if changes need to be made, and they are not your AA's, such as missing words, sentences, or typos made by the typesetter, these should not be billable.

Be consistent in your writing style. Every author has a style. Nurture yours and be consistent. If you choose to make a point with italics — stick to that format, don't suddenly switch to outline format. If you choose to include subheads in your chapters, don't bounce back and forth from all caps to upper and lower case. If you choose to use the word "website," don't suddenly mention a "web site." Just about anything goes when it comes to "your" style — as long as you're consistent.

And finally, about typos. This is a very scary word to a typesetter, especially after the book has been printed and you have to look at it 1,000 or 100,000 times — but it's inevitable. I have yet to see a perfect book — any-where — ever. The best you can do is to avoid the "biggies." Believe it or not, many authors, so intent on the text of the book, forget to READ the covers. Read the covers (front and back) — especially the title and your name — say every letter out loud. A mistake on the covers unfortunately requires a reprint. Other areas often missed are the title page, dedication, acknowledgements, the copyright page, contents, running heads, chapter titles and subtitles, and captions. Check these very carefully as they will be the first to get noticed. A typo hidden in the text of a paragraph is often never read as a typo — sometimes, miraculously, our minds insert the proper word — so that's not as bad. But no matter what, typos are best avoided, so proofread carefully. And if you're not confident about your proofreading abilities, hire a professional. A typesetter should never be a proof-reader; they're just too close to the words.

Occasionally, and we hope this is rare, a typo gets printed — now what? All designers/typesetters will insist you sign off on proofs before they are sent to the printer. You, as the author/publisher have the final say. Once you approve the proofs, you assume all the responsibility for its content. If there are typos, you need to understand that you also assume the expense of reprinting if it is required. This is the industry standard. If it weren't this way — no one would ever set type.

And don't forget; ask for a copy of the disk when your book is complete. This is invaluable if you need reprints. Keep it in a safe place."

*Stephanie Ward, President*
*TeleSet, Inc., Hillsborough, NJ*

When you start your interview process for a cover designer and typesetter, you must have some basic knowledge of what is involved from a cost standpoint. You will find above the basic details needed by the expert to properly represent you. But let's face it, how much will you have to pay?

Each professional has a different way to determine how much to charge you, but the basic system involves distinct, very specific methodology. If you are really green behind the gills and need more "hands-on" work, then of course the price should include fees for such assistance. Again, if you don't know what font size to use or paper color or print darkness, etc., your expert can help greatly with thoughts on what should be used. On the other hand, if you know all that but have no idea how to put a cover together, you should only have to pay for such expertise.

Charges normally include a fee for the cover itself and the more work needed, the higher the price you should pay. If you give him/her several photos to put on the front and back, layout is critical, and money should be paid. Presume that you will use an illustration or two, or maybe some fine art work. Again, you get what you pay for.

The production cost for the interior of the book can be even more complicated to estimate. The amount of time needed often creates the high or low here. But if you don't need much help on the other technicalities, the basic charge comes down to "How much per page?" and in the case of photos — "How much to scan each photo/illustration?"

Your typesetting needs could be filled with ease and the cost generally comes down to dollars per printed page. So if your book will run 128 pages after all is said and done, the price will probably include so much for the cover and so much per page. A wide range of $10-15 per page is the ballpark you will be in for the interior and the cover charge is even more unpredictable. In any case, don't go with the lowest priced quote unless you are dead certain that this firm is one capable of giving you expert and quick service. Buying the "cheapest" could be a huge error indeed!

Besides cover and per page charges, understand that you will probably have to also pay for postage, shipping, faxes, long distance telephone calls, etc. Unless you are in driving range, lots of money will have to be charged to get printed material to and from you for proof reading. On the other hand, if you have expertise with email, you may be able to avoid some of these charges.

And of importance is the need to know if any state taxes are to be paid. The designer/typesetter doesn't earn the money so they may forget to even tell you what charge they have to pass on to government, but it still comes out of your pocket so check this point out when you get your quotes.

This one is tricky, by the way, and that's why we discuss getting a good accountant a few chapters from now. As a basic rule of thumb, you don't pay taxes to any provider, nor do you collect taxes from a wholesaler or retailer because they are responsible for this. But you certainly must collect and pay taxes for books that you sell directly to consumers in most states.

# CHAPTER TWO

# Getting It
# Printed/Published

## HARD VERSUS SOFT COVER

U nless you are writing a textbook, or something that really lends itself better to schools or libraries, having your book printed in hardcover is more for you than anyone else. Let's face it, a hard cover book is more permanent. If you are looking to make a permanent mark in history, then have it done that way. And that is a really great idea if people buy it, and if you have the money to lay out beforehand for such a printing. Be very careful before you make a decision to go hard cover first and then into soft because the cost may doom your project to failure. Unless you are highly skilled in marketing and unless you have written a book that lends itself better to hard, honestly, you may be better served to go soft and save the extra money for publicity and advertising.

You are the publisher, in whatever name or identity you seek to use, but someone has to print the book for you, and you may underestimate just how complicated a topic this can be.

As just noted in the prior chapter, the charge to get a book printed could include hidden fees that the printer just passes on to you. They normally tell you what they intend to collect for their services, monies that will go into their treasury, but you must know what monies they will have to get and pass on to other facilities.

The biggest hidden charge besides tax is shipping! The printer will typically mail "blue-lines" to you to review. (Today, however, laser proofs are becoming the norm.) This is the large set of printed pages that make up the actual book, before it gets to be a book. Traditionally, the printer sends your book to you in this form so that you can make the final proofreading of it before giving them the actual go-ahead.

Once you receive the blue-lines, hopefully you will not find any author's errors, because changes at this stage of the game are extremely expensive and can delay your schedule.

Back and forth shipping and other mail charges are normally passed on to the publisher, and that, dear reader, is you, so know about it and make sure you include such expenses when determining what you will have to pay for the entire project. Remember too that the overall cost to you plays a huge part in how much you should show as a cover price as well!

## CARTON WEIGHT AND COUNT

While talking about shipping, let's make sure we know who you are and what you are capable of. You also have to consider to whom you will try to sell the book. Two general subjects wrap up together here, carton weight and unloading. Most printers will not put more than 40 pounds of books in a single container, but you cannot assume this. Make sure what you are getting. If you are a lightweight and cannot handle 40 pounds with ease, tell the printer to not put more than, for example, 30 pounds per box, or so many books in each. Buyers like to know how many books are in each carton because (let's hope you get such orders), the bigger sources buy by the full box, rather than in tens and twenties.

A carton of 80 books containing 128 pages might hit that 40-pound mark and be a good tight package. But you may only want a 30-pound box and that might only carry 60 books. In this instance, the printer might stuff a 40-pound box with 60 books and those little Styrofoam® "peanuts" to make a full carton. That's good for you because you can hold onto the packing material for future use. And another weight problem can take place if the trucker that your printer selects will not bring the load right to your door AND unload for you. You might come home one day and find fifty cases of books plopped down on the ground right out in the open, exposed to weather or theft. So make sure you have them shipped REQUIRING your signature, and in cartons you can handle, as well as brought to your door. (A tip to the driver couldn't hurt either if you want him/her to carry them into the house.)

## PRINTER INFORMATION

Strictly so that you can have a brief shopping list of where you can outreach to for quotes on the production of your book, here are a few places for you to contact. For more names, check Dan Poynter's book.

In alphabetical order, they are:

■ **BookMasters, Inc.** in Ohio — call 800-537-6727 or by fax, try 419-589-4040. They printed three of my books.

■ **Lithoid Printing Corp.** is in New Jersey, and also printed three of my books. Call them at 908-238-4000. Their fax number is 908-238-9628.

■ **Omnipress** is a firm situated in Wisconsin and I spoke to Bob Hamm. His number is 800-828-0305 if you are calling from out of state and the fax is 608-246-4237.

■ **Rose Printing** can be found in Florida and Gary Alford told me that they print 2,500 or so books yearly. Call them for quotes at 800-227-3725 or by fax, 850-576-4153.

When you seek quotes from any printer, you need to know in advance what you really want. For example, are you going with soft or hardcover? Is time critical? Make sure you explain that to the account executive. The type of binding will determine cost variables, as will the colors in the cover. Typically, "four-color" is quite nice, but also expensive.

When you start your outreach to printers for quotes, make sure you know the "fine print" in advance. Just as another example, are you obliged to buy the number of extra books that are printed or can you refuse to do so?

All printers will give you a quote but here again comes the devil "fine print." For example, "overruns." As a rule, most printers will quote on your order of, say 2,500 copies, but will also tell you how much you will have to pay for "overs." Generally, any such additional books printed will be at bargain prices, but if your budget doesn't allow for same, know in advance that you must discuss this with the printer.

You see, the printing presses run and run and more copies than specified are always printed, in case of damage during the folding and binding process. Separate printing is done of your book covers and here again, not as an exact science. Therefore know that some printers will oblige you to buy extra books printed, subject to a realistic maximum number of, for example, 10% extra.

On the other hand, some printers will allow you to tell them that you ONLY want an exact number printed. And still others will actually allow you the luxury of receiving a supply of the extra covers that they might otherwise have simply thrown away.

Extra covers can be wonderful sales tools for you so when you are talking to printers, ask them if they can so accommodate you. This is discussed later in the book, but just remember, "Can I get extra covers?" and "Can I only buy an exact number of books?" are big questions you should ask of any printer you talk to.

# ADVICE FROM A PRINTER

As we heard some words of wisdom from my designer/typesetter, let's hear some now from Ray Sevin, President of BookMasters, Inc., of Ohio, the company that printed my last three books. If you decide to honor them with a call for a quote for your book, make sure to make at least a few more calls as well.

"In beginning the process of self-publishing, two major expectations must be clearly defined. The first are your own expectations and the second are those of the book manufacturer.

Communicating your own expectations begins with a detailed, accurate estimate request. Although there may be some very good generic request forms available, BookMasters strongly suggests a visit to the manufacturer's website. Each manufacturer will have slight differences in the questions they require you to answer. If you are unfamiliar with the terminology then you should speak to a salesman. If you do not wish to do either, send a book from your own library (which should be returned to you) that you want your book fashioned after.

Once the manufacturer provides you with an estimate it is your responsibility to question any and all items you do not understand. Acceptance of the estimate, with the details therein, will be applied to the job ticket from which your project will be manufactured.

Make sure that you understand the process your project will follow. Again, each manufacturer may do things a little differently. Never assume that what one printer has done for you will automatically be done by another printer. There are very specific steps that YOU are responsible for in order to maintain your schedule needs and completion date. It is the responsibility of the printer to explain their expectations of you in this process.

Before sending your electronic files or camera ready copy to the printer, make sure that you are doing so as spelled out on your quotation. Any deviation from the quotation will most likely result in additional cost to you. Electronic files must be submitted per the requirements of the individual printer. Once again, these instructions should be available on their website. If you are not capable of submitting files either in QuarkXPress or PageMaker, it would be best to send "camera ready copy" (clean, corrected lasers). Proofread NOW, not later! Corrections after this stage will be very costly and will most likely affect your schedule. If you must make corrections after you receive your proofs from the printer, send the corrections in the same manner as the original copy; lasers for lasers, electronic files for electronic files.

Return your proofs promptly or your schedule will suffer. Color proofs of your cover will more than likely NOT match your color lasers if you provided your cover electronically. If color is ABSOLUTELY critical most printers will suggest that you have color film produced locally where you can inspect and color-correct and send the approved color proof and film to the printer. Another option is to allow the printer to create the color film for you from the original artwork. However, you can still expect some color variation from proof to final product depending on the protective coating being applied to the cover.

If you and your printer are clear on these expectations and are communicating without assuming, your experience should be a good one. Book manufacturing is a mechanical process of ink on paper, folders, gathering machines, coaters, binders, and trimmers. All of these have certain tolerances. Possibly the biggest expectation that will have to be compromised is that of absolute perfection. Expect good quality and a saleable product but understand that printing and binding is not a perfect science."

*Ray Sevin, President*
*BookMasters, Inc., Ohio*

Well, that about sums up what a printer expects from you and, frankly, I'm glad I called Ray and asked him to spell it all out. Of course if you have a really good typesetter and designer, he/she will know most of that, but Mr. Sevin just answered many questions you may have had.

I had one book printed in New Jersey and had reprints of three books done by that same firm. That printer kept my negatives for me as a convenience, and then they went out of business, taking my negatives down the dumper with them. (This was not Lithoid, of course.) We talked before about "backing up" in a variety of ways. If you buy cheap, you might also wind up losing your printer someday so "Caveat Emptor" (let the buyer beware), and no matter what, back it up!

Technically, the negatives are your property. Ask for them (a minimal cost may apply) if you plan to re-print or have any misgivings about the printer.

To repeat, if you buy cheap, you might also wind up losing your printer someday!

And now here's something that can really confuse a novice author, and for the majority of you who knew it already, please remember that we are working to help everyone, beginners, and folks who know a bit more too. So my apologies to you who knew, but for the others, a bit of advice that you will understand quickly, but may not have grasped unless you read it first here...

## VOLUME PURCHASE

When you outreach for quotes, just about every printer will give you prices based on a variety of multiples. If your book is to contain 128 pages, has four-color covers, and is to be printed on good quality stock, your price might be in the range of $1 to $2 each copy for 5,000 copies. If you only want 3,000 copies the printers probably will quote more per book, in the vicinity of $1.25 to $2.50 each. They also will give you prices for "additional thousands', more than likely, at even better figures.

Say the next 1,000 books will be at $1 each if you went from 5,000 to 6,000 or at $1.25 each to jump up to 4,000 copies in lieu of 3,000.

So you go with a print run of either 5,000 or 3,000 and save the quote, to later realize that you were successful even quicker than you thought and now you call up the printer and ask for the next thousand at the lower price originally quoted. And again, my apologies for those who have more brain function than I did way back when. You see, when I was about to run out of inventory for my first book, I assumed that the next thousand would cost me the price that was quoted originally. Hypothetically speaking, go with a first run of 3,000 at, say $2.50, each. I assumed that the next thousand would be at, say $1.25, each. And boy, was I wrong!

When you do a re-order a year or two later, the printer may have all the original data on hand. But even if the price of paper has not gone up, or labor remains the same, they still will have to charge more per copy because their volume discounts apply for real volume, each time, not for the aggregate number printed over the years. So if you want another thousand copies now, not only will you not get the $1.25 price, you will probably have to pay more than the original $2.50 each, because discounts are built into selling you inventory based on a continuous press run. If you only order a run of 1,000, the unit cost goes up! Therefore it is important to not under buy. While you may take a while longer to sell off stock, clearly, your price per copy will be far less in such instances!

A few other services might also be available to you from

your printer, and in some cases, may be of extreme importance to you. Therefore, when looking for prices, ask what other options they can offer to you. Just as an example, some printers have vast warehouses in which they might be willing to store a majority of your books for you. If you order 5,000 copies and pay for them, you may not yet be equipped to store them in your garage or basement. And if you are an apartment dweller, you certainly don't have the room. Yes, you can rent space or ask a friend or relative, but storing your books for you by the printer is a wonderful feature to take advantage of, if the need exists.

Remember, books need to be stored in a cool, dry place — musty smelling, warped books won't sell well!

Some printers will store but charge for storage. Watch this one, because the price can build up quickly. Just be sure to seek an answer to this question from your prospective printer in case you have such a need. By the way, if they do store for you, once you need more inventory, the books don't just appear magically at your door. Someone sends them to you and a charge occurs. So be on notice that there are a few additional costs that you may not have considered along the way.

Your printer will usually be glad to send books for you to your bulk-buying customers also. So if they are warehousing books and Bookazine, for example, wants two boxes, it might cost more for the printer to ship for you, but in the long run, your at home inventory won't be reduced and this could make a lot of sense. In all cases, be certain you know how much is charged for shipping and storage!

Now that you have lined up your printer, what else?

## WHERE TO START

Earlier on, we talked about how to write your book. Let's get into it a bit more now. Presuming you haven't even begun to write your book yet, let's review things. A non-fiction book is not difficult to produce, if you know your subject. It really doesn't matter too much either if the subject has already been written about. Let's face it, there are very few hobbies, sports, foods, outdoor topics, languages, ethnic groups, etc., that are out there that haven't been written about. You should view this as a positive rather than a negative. After all, if someone has written about the thing you know best, you might be able to write a better book about it! So use the fact that it's "been done" and go write your own book!

The simple solution to producing a book is to have first-hand knowledge of the material and also the capability to conduct research, thereby accumulating a substantial volume of additional data. Regarding research, here are some ideas:

■ **Libraries.** Clearly, the first place is your local library. If it is not a very big facility, expand your horizon a bit and pay a visit to several nearby, bigger ones too.

Librarians, by their very nature, are wonderfully cooperative individuals. They all are well educated and are extremely well read. Most are far from outgoing, but I have yet to meet one that doesn't go out of their way to respond to questions. Again, depending on the size of the library, you can get assistance from, generally speaking, the Reference Librarian. This person has computer access and card file documentation to direct you to tons of material that can be found on the topic you seek to gain additional knowledge about.

While a book or two may be on the shelves of your library about your subject, the Reference Librarian can probably point you to other areas. Magazines in particular are wonderful sources of data. Nearly all libraries have vast computer banks of knowledge. If you have the ability to look into the library's computer bank and glean items of interest on your topic, all the better. However, if you pick a quiet day (not a Saturday, of course), and find the reference person not too busy, ask for help. Kind words and attitude go a very long way here!

Magazine articles on your subject matter can be used to further your knowledge, but don't hesitate to quote from them also. For example, when I co-wrote "Gone Fishin' With Kids" with my friend Joe Perrone, I went to the library and looked up fishing magazines and read all the stories I could find about taking kids fishing. Taking a sentence or two out of several of these articles, being careful to quote the source and name the author, adds credibility to your book, as well as making it more informative to the reader.

■ **Bookstores.** The bigger the better, but don't omit specialty shops. If you are writing about something that has its own particular niche, like gay, ethnic, porn, etc., then go to such stores to seek further knowledge. If no specialty bookstores exist, then you might be better served to go bigger. Just remember that if you are looking for help from an employee in the store, the less crowded, the better. Avoid evenings that are typically active like Thursdays, and stay away like the plague from mall stores on Saturday and Sunday. Common sense applies. Besides browsing through other topical books, you may find that the young worker with earrings and tattoos in the strangest of places may be your best source for ideas on where to gather material.

■ **Clubs.** If clubs exist in connection with your topic, and you don't belong, by all means, climb on board quickly. If none are nearby, join anyway, and get on their mailing lists. The material covered in club newsletters can provide you with gobs of useful detail. If you can find clubs that are within an hour or two drive, make it your business to not only join but attend meetings as well. In addition to gathering data, you will have a ready audience of willing buyers for your book this way as soon as you publish it! And, of course, offer to write pieces for their newsletter without compensation in exchange for advertising space for your book. You may even want to tell them that you will donate a buck or two to the club out of receipts produced from identifiable club member purchases. Last but not least, if they don't have a newsletter, offer to put one out for them on a quarterly basis to start.

■ **The internet.** If you have any technical skill at all, you may find out that the best source of knowledge can be accessed with your own computer. If you are not already set up to access the internet, most libraries offer free usage of the internet. Simply go to a "search engine" such as www.yahoo.com and enter the words relevant to your subject in the search box.

## THE COVER PRICE?

Now that you have done so much research into costs, how about figuring out what to charge for your book? Start first with a cover price, but realize that you personally don't get anywhere near that amount for your effort. You have to deduct the production costs, discounts you must offer to wholesalers, distributors, and retailers, as well as the vast shipping charges you will be hit with.

And worst of all might be the price you will have to pay for returns. A return is the dirtiest of all words to a publisher! You see, in nearly all instances of sales to the big guys, you must agree to allow them to be reimbursed for books that they cannot sell, or that they get back from the retailers they sold the books to. That word, "return" gets your knees knocking quite loud and while it is a cost of doing business, it can hurt badly. Some wholesalers will tell you that they will not stick you with a return charge-back if some of the books they send back to you are in one manner or another, damaged. But others will say that if you want them to try to sell your books, you have to eat any and all books they send back to you and you must give them back the full price they paid to you for the inventory. They may also demand that you reimburse them for their return shipping charges back to you.

My personal experiences with both Ingram and Bookazine were relatively pleasant on this subject, and other wholesalers might be okay too. Both allow me to tell them about certain books that they return which just could not be placed back into inventory. If a retail store places a store sticker on the back which cannot be removed without causing damage, than that book becomes little more than a donation to charity for you. Worse, if the retailer sends the books back to the wholesaler with bent or torn pages or covers, maybe with dirt, the book cannot be sold. So when selecting your wholesaler, you really need to have a clear understanding of what is and what is not "returnable." If you know what you have to accept back and it sounds fair to you, then you have an idea of what pitfalls lie in your path on this complex topic.

Another option is to have the printer shrink-wrap each book, especially if it is hardcover or expensive to produce. This adds protection and adds to the cost, but it may be worth it to you. You may also consider having a portion of the run wrapped or have a few wrapped locally (if your distributor is sloppy).

When Ingram sends books back to you, they also include an "Unacceptable Return Expedite Form" within the package. This form is provided to publishers in case they feel that Ingram wants to get credit for returned books that are in a condition that makes them unsaleable. They ask you to look at the returned books and tell them which books were either not yours, or sent back with bent, crumpled or dirty pages, with glue residue, etc. Chances are quite good that if you are reasonable with them, they will be reasonable with you, and will tell you that they want a reduced credit instead based on your list of legitimate complaints. Bookazine has also agreed to reduce their request for return credit when I was able to convince them that part of their demand was not in order. My guess is that some other wholesalers will also be fair on this.

On the other hand, some wholesalers will tell you that if you want to sell to them, you will have to accept ALL "returns" with no questions asked. You will have to give them full credit and may even have to pay for the return shipping cost. As noted, some wholesalers do not make you "eat" all returns and others do so. While selling to these companies be 100% positive about who requires what and who doesn't! Like they say, "Caveat Venditor" (Let the seller beware.)

You see, pricing the book is not just about how much you paid to get it printed vs. how much you can sell it for. Returns can dramatically mess up any such formula.

Presume that you ran 5,000 copies and your overall cost was $10,000 for typesetting, printing and all other production charges. Since your unit cost was $2.00, what should you show as the cover price? Well, start with the biggest discount you may have to allow and work out from there. You may be forced to give a 65% discount, maybe more, to a distributor. Just for example, start with a $10 retail price and let's work the numbers together. If you are going to give 65% off, on the $10 book, you will wind up with only $3.50, and that doesn't even include shipping and return costs. While some readers will buy from you at retail, your best average income would really be more like 50% of the cover price.

The wholesalers generally want 55% off. They normally allow 40% off to the retail stores they supply and the other 15% is a fair income for them to receive. You will probably get 60% of the cover price for sales directly to the traditional retail bookstores. (Offer them autographed copies as a further inducement to buy directly from you.)

If you are going to average 50% of the cover price as your income, and that may be on the high side, then $5.00 income compared to $2.00 cost sounds pretty good, but again, the devil "Return" rears its ugly head once more. And what about unsold inventory too? You have to sell at least 20-30% of what you paid for before you get into the black!

Selecting your cover price is quite critical and can make or break you. For the most part, you should be able to average at least three times your costs for sales. Hey, if you add in a unit price for all the time and effort you put into researching and writing the book, based on what you make per hour in your regular line of work you may think that the whole idea of writing a book makes no sense at all. But of course we writers don't do that because, if we did, no one would ever write a book again!

There are some publishers who won't even put a cover price on the book at all, preferring to have a "suggested" retail price instead that they tell people about. Some like to show the cover price on the top right-hand side of the back cover and others want it on the bottom right. If the price sounds high, the argument goes that top right may scare off a buyer, but my preference still is top right.

Do you round off a price or not? The bigger retail store chains have spent tons of money on research regarding this topic. Just go into one of the "mart" type stores that are near you and pick up a variety of products that cost $10 or more each. More than likely, you will see that they priced the box at a number that either ends at 95 or 99 cents! Instead of $15.00, they label it at $14.95 or $14.99. Don't laugh at this one. Hundreds of thousands of research dollars went into convincing retailers to show one of these 90-cent numbers at the end. Hey, on its face, doesn't $9.99 sound at first like a much lower number than $10.00 to you? No? Well you are right, but don't try to tell a chain store guy that. When you are telling someone about the bargain that you bought, don't you sometimes drop the last few numbers? If the TV cost $459, haven't you heard someone say it only cost a little over $400?

Some retailers have non-bending ground rules here. If they want to show 99 cents at the end and your price shows at $12.95, they may actually be obliged to mark your book down to $11.99 to stick with their in-house marketing rules.

Spend time on this before you decide on a price. Just figuring how much of a multiple of costs you want to get is not enough. Truthfully, while the number of pennies shown at the end is of little importance in the scheme of things, it may have real meaning later on.

If you have doubts about how much to show as your price, then increase it by a dollar instead of reducing it. Unless you are looking for a specific kind of number, like $9.99 or $19.99, add a buck. Instead of $12.95 change it to $13.95. No one will know that you first thought about $12.95, and if they are going to buy it, they will spend the $13+ just as quickly as they would go for $12+! And your overall profit will increase substantially also.

## MORE NUMBERS

Did you think you are all done with numbers now that you are done with determining what to charge? Well, far from it, because more numbers are needed, as many as three sets of them! And if you don't get this right, you may be exposing yourself to a far greater number of returns later on, returns that cannot be re-sold. These numbers are those that you find on the back cover of just about every product sold everywhere! These numbers are also printed on your copyright page. They are, in order:

■ **ISBN.** This is an International Standard Book Number and virtually every library and conventional bookstore MUST know what your ISBN is, or else they will probably not want to buy your book! Inventory control of every sophisticated level demands this. The most basic systems as well as the ones that are most complicated require everyone in bookstores and libraries to know what the ISBN is!

You can get your own ISBN number by contacting International Standard Book Number, U. S. Agency — R.R. Bowker, 121 Chanlon Rd., New Providence, NJ 07974. Or call Bowker at 877-310-7333 or 888-269-5372. A relatively modest fee is charged and you can order a set of ISBN's in varying multiples, based on how many books you expect to ultimately produce. I bought a set of 10 in 1994 and this book is my ninth self-published work, leaving me with one number left to use. Sets are available in multiples of 10, 100, 1,000 and 10,000. You will need to apply a different ISBN for each edition of your work so if you are going to print it hardcover and soft, and put an audiotape out, etc, you have already used up three of a set of ten. Therefore, you may want to go for 100 uses instead of 10. Frankly, that was what I should have done in 1994!

Your designer/typesetter will place your ISBN number on the back cover of the book, as well as on the copyright page. The last few numbers are the only ones that change. Just remember to have your designer/typesetter use a different suffix number every time you produce another book.

To be specific, take for example the ISBN number for this book, 0-9650261-8-3. The suffix, 8-3, identifies this book and counts as one of the 10 uses for the ISBN number 0-9650261. If I were to market a hardcover version, I would assign my last ISBN # 0-9650261-9-1 counting it as my last of the 10 uses.

■ **UPC.** A Universal Product Code number is what the conventional specialty stores — drug store, supermarket, sporting goods, etc. — wanted to see on each book. They set up their computers with the need to know every product number. Not many years ago, you couldn't even get anyone to buy your book without a UPC number on it. And if they did buy them without such a number appearing, then the store would put a store sticker on the book with their own store number on it. Returns of such books nearly always created junk for you because the stickers damaged the book in the process of trying to remove them!

To get your own UPC number, call the Uniform Code Council in Dayton, OH. At 1-800-543-8137.

■ **Bookland EAN Barcode.** This stands for European

Article Number and it has replaced the UPC number in many retail facilities, at least those that are bookstores. Every nickel and dime cash register has computer control that will "scan" your book and this bar code number tells the computer how much to charge for it. The Bookland bar code number is an offshoot of the ISBN, to be discussed further shortly.

To get the imprinted numbers for your book, contact any of the bar code suppliers that are found in Dan Poynter's book. Two of them are: **Fotel, Inc.,** Lomard, IL, 1-800-834-4920; and **J & D Barcodes,** Glendora, CA 1-626-914-1777.

I used Fotel for my last three books and they were not only helpful and quite responsive, but inexpensive too. Reaching out to them for assistance in describing numbering systems, they wrote:

"Bookland EAN barcodes are derived from the ISBN number or International Standard Book Number. This code is the bookstore equivalent to the UPC barcode or Universal Product Code. All Bookland EAN barcodes start with the number "978" which denotes Bookland, and then the ISBN can be traced digit for digit until the last digit which is a mathematically generated self-checking digit for the scanning device. An example would be an ISBN number 0-1234567-8-9 which would become 9780123456786. The last digit of the ISBN and the last digit of the Bookland EAN barcode will not be the same in most instances, although in some cases, the check digit (*) matches. Many times, price extensions or addendum barcodes associated with the Bookland EAN barcode are used. This second set of bars encodes the retail price of the book which, when scanned, will reflect the price encoded to the scanning system. US prices are encoded with a preceding "5" and then the retail price follows. For instance, to encode

(*) The "check digit" is the last digit in both the EAN and ISBN.

$12.95, the price addendum would read 51295. To not encode a price, but maintain the addendum format, one should encode "90000" in the price code."

*Kevin Sousa, Manager*
*Fotel, Inc., IL*

Remember that your ability to sell requires you to have as many numbers as possible on the back of the book. Price? Yes, but ISBN, UPC and EAN also can't hurt!

Once you have all your numbers in place, get back to Bowker again, but at a different location, to get your book listed in the most important directory around. It is called "Books in Print" and it is published yearly each October. This book is the ultimate bible for stores and libraries all across the world. Write to Advance Book Information, R.R. Bowker Data Collection Center, Box 6000, Oldsmar, FL 34677-6800, and ask for an ABI form. This form is to be completed by you and it tells Bowker, who then tells everyone else about your book. Besides the computer methods that have evolved, there is nothing better for you to do, promotion wise, at so little cost, than to get your book into "Books In Print®!" Just remember to tell them if and when you move or change telephone numbers, etc., in order to let them have current details.

The last few pages of this book (Appendix A) have a copy of the Advance Book Information Form for your convenience.

## COPYRIGHT INFORMATION

According to the US Government, "copyright protection subsists from the time the work is created in fixed form. The copyright in the work of authorship immediately becomes the property of the author who created the work. Only the author or those deriving their rights through the author can rightfully claim copyright." The copyright lasts the author's lifetime plus 70 years after the author's death, and ownership can transfer to heirs. A copyright is automatic when a work is created, whether it is published or not, as long as it contains the following three elements:

1. The symbol © (the letter C in a circle), or the word "Copyright," or the abbreviation "Copr.;" and
2. The year of first publication of the work; and
3. The name of the owner of copyright in the work, or an abbreviation by which the name can be recognized.

Example: © 2002 Emanuel Luftglass

In general, copyright registration is a legal formality intended to make a public record of the basic facts of a particular copyright. Registration is not required for copyright protection, but a formal registration will provide you with certain legal advantages in the case of copyright infringement, and it only costs about $30.00. For additional information, request Publication No. 563 "How to Protect Your Intellectual Property Right," from: **U.S. Customs Service,** P.O. Box 7404, Washington, D.C. 20044 or on the internet, go to www.loc.gov/copyright/ for all the info and forms you need.

# CHAPTER THREE

# Going Into Business

Let's face it, if you are serious about this book-writing thing, you have to go about it the right way. Besides writing a good book, you also must know how to conduct yourself as a business owner. Clearly, you have an advantage if you already are a merchant, but whatever you do, to "sell books" requires a working knowledge of how to run a business.

Somewhere along the way, perhaps even before you sit down and put the first chapter of your book together, you should make an appointment with a good accountant. You really need to know what it takes and this would be one place to start. Of course, if you have someone doing your taxes now, a full time practitioner (not someone trying to make a few extra dollars working for a bucket shop), talk to that person.

For example, you will need to know how to deal with state taxes on the sale of your books. If your state charges tax, whom do you collect it from and whom not? If you sell to a library, the answer is no. If you sell to a store, it can go either way. You may not have to collect if they charge tax to their ultimate consumer because double taxation is not required in nearly all instances. But you will probably be required to get tax I.D. numbers from all the stores that you sell to so that "big brother" can make sure that those stores charge and pay taxes. On the other hand, if you sell to an individual directly, then you will probably be required to collect and pay taxes to your state.

Don't fool around with this one. Consult a good account-ant to make sure you are walking the straight and narrow. If you are in a state that has its own taxes (a few still exist that don't, honest), a call to the state itself might be another way to handle things but again, our advice is to get your own pro-fessional to help you out.

When "selling," it is far better to have an identity other than "Jane Doe." Few storeowners will buy from an individual, so early on, establish a trade name that you feel properly repre-sents you and what you are doing. Since my origin is in the writing of fishing books, then the trade name, "Gone Fishin' Enterprises" fits my needs well.

For name selection, ask your accountant how to go about it, and you may also want to discuss this with an attorney. An attorney can help you form a corporation and a corporate name may be what you want. This can be more expensive, but you have less liability when you have a corporation.

The single most important thing to discuss with your accountant is what you can and what you cannot "write off!" Travel to and from the topic you are writing about is gen-erally an easy "write off," as are fees that you pay to enter or participate in the subject matter. Food that you buy is not as easy to deduct, because, after all, you have to eat anyway, right? But you should be able to deduct the costs over and above normal food charges.

In another of the many fine features that Jeffery D. Zbar wrote for *WD*, this time in its December 2001 issue, he tells readers to avoid waiting until their taxes are due before making up a tax plan. Well, of course that's true, but have you ever watched television the night of April 15th and seen the folks sitting on the ground at the main branch of the New York City Post Office, with papers strewn all around them? Chances are you have, but don't let anything like that happen to you. Plan well in advance for the tax implications you will be faced with in your business, with your accountant and attorney, so that you can take advantage of each and every "write-off" the government allows you to take.

While the money you pay to your printer, designer/type-setter, etc., are clear deductions, only your accountant can tell you what you may deduct when it is time to pay federal and state income taxes.

Writing a book can be fun, but you may as well look at it in the long run as going into a business, and in that, quite a few benefits can also be derived.

Can you deduct the cost of your computer? Ask the accountant to be sure. Maybe a portion of its cost? Ask! The cost of the disks that you write the book on and the paper that you use to print it on are easy deductions. But how about your telephone? If you use it to get prices for the book, do research, interview staff, etc., deduct those costs, obviously, but keep good, accurate records!

Some people deduct the entire cost of the room they use for writing, sales, etc., calling that an "office" deduction, but your accountant may advise against doing so. Face it, if you have an eight-room house you really can't take $\frac{1}{8}$ of all the houses' costs off your tax return. You cannot unless you can factually prove that the room in question was not needed or used or existed before you sat down to write that great work of literature you are involved with.

# CHAPTER FOUR

# Partnership

Make a decision very carefully here, because if you had not thought about entering into such a venture before you bought this book, you really might be angry with me because I suggested it! Honestly, a partnership in most anything is often doomed to fail. It usually is a matter of time before such a "marriage" breaks up, but if you really are both careful and lucky, and work at making it work, a partnership would be one way for you to have a far better chance at success with your book.

Picking a partner is not something you do haphazardly. If you are already close to someone who knows your subject matter well, and you may have already discussed it with her/him, proceed carefully with formulating a game plan. It is far easier to write a book by yourself as a rule, but what about getting it printed? And how can you get someone to buy it? What if you are great at research and know your topic like the back of your hand but are not skilled in writing? If the concept of "selling" makes your knees go wobbly, and you cannot find a good agent or representative to do this for you, than you really might need a partner.

Regardless of how close two people may be, it is probable that half of all partnerships break up.

Fortunately, and luck played a big part in these experiences for me, I wrote two books with my closest fishing buddy and one with another good friend. We all are still close, and I never had any doubts about producing each book as a joint venture. Both friends are more skilled in writing then I am, while I am better at selling! And my primary career in the insurance business reached substantial success because I went into a partnership with a co-worker and we still are the closest of friends. (On the other hand, don't ask me about the bank and newspaper partnerships that I was part of — they don't make pretty stories.)

My advice to you is to write your own book, get it printed, and handle your own marketing, if you think you can do it and have the time to handle it. Arguments will be limited, while in a partnership they could become limitless! By the way, a partnership MUST be entered into regarding your project with your significant other, if you have such a partner, in any event.

A marriage or other such arrangement can be tested rather strenuously if you decide on your own to just sit down and write a book without agreement from the other half of your household! ("You are going to spend how much money?") And how about "Don't tell me we can't go on vacation because you are stuck with that %$@doggone*_+ book!"

Co-venturing with your significant other can also be a way to go and it might be either the easiest or worst way to try it out. Marriage alone is tough but adding another dimension like writing a book together can really be brutal.

A partnership can work well if you plan together and agree on who does what and how much time will be committed to the project by each partner. Writing the book together is rough enough but you have to decide how to pay for the book, and what to do with income when it arrives.

If, for example, one partner has no money and the other lays it all out (printing, production, advertising), then clearly, the money spender might be the one who should get more of the profit, if such a bonanza were to take place. On the other hand, if #1 pays for it but #2 writes most of the book, what do you do then? Another scenario could involve the sales that occur after a year or two passes. If Baker & Taylor, Bookazine, etc., kicks out a purchase order two years after you published the book, who gets how much of the income then? And worst of all, what if an enormous box of books come back as "returns?" This matter can create panic if new sales are not taking place, because the wholesaler wants their money back and doesn't much care who pays them. So you must know in advance how to split this expense.

If one partner handles most of the sales later on, how do you cut up the income? This too needs to be decided on. One of my books was written with a good friend who moved far away, but we still split the income. In this case, we had decided early on that the one who closed on a specific sale got 75% of the income, and renewal sales to that source went down to a 60/40% split. Unsolicited book sale income was divided equally. Again, even if it is your very closest buddy, you must establish ground rules very carefully. Forgetting the book itself, the last thing you want to do is break up a close friendship and that often is what takes place because of a joint venture.

Advice from your accountant and attorney could be invaluable. To be best represented, separate professionals may be the way to go. A single accountant is less risky, but two attorneys really should be selected. Consult with all of them too regarding whether to do this via the partnership route or by forming a corporation.

Forming a partnership and what to do during its existence may very well be more trouble than it's worth, but, as stated above, if you are careful and lucky, your project could wind up far more successful.

# CHAPTER FIVE

# The Basics

## BOOK DESIGN

So you want to write a book? Get in line! Or at least get in line trying to get someone to buy it once it comes out.

You see, as many as 50% of the people who have graduated from a college and are at least 40 years of age want to write one too! Many have already done so, but few have actually gotten the book published. I dare say that more than 25% of the rest of the population who have any manner of education at all also have a book idea. If a person can spell, or owns a computer that has a simple spell check program, she too may already be thinking about a book.

Before we continue to talk more about how to write one, let's throw some gauntlets in your path — things that you will need to know about at some time during the process.

In no particular order, how about these?

■ **Cover design.** Oh, "you can't tell a book by its cover?" That may be true, but most people who buy books that they never heard of do just that. If the cover attracts them, it at least creates interest.

■ **Book dimensions.** Standard "pocket book" size is 5½ inches wide by 8½ inches high. But really, if you go into any bookstore, you will see books in every conceivable set of dimensions. Whatever your subject matter, it is very important to make an early decision about this topic. If you want your book to go into the typical display rack, it must fit! This book measures 6 x 9 as do the eight other books that I self-published. However, the two we did for Rutgers University Press measured 5½ by 8½ .

■ **Letter quality.** Important decisions need to be made here, based on who you hope will buy your book. The darkness of print? Yes, especially if your target market involves very young or old readers. Select carefully when you determine what size the letters should be and how dark they are to appear. Your computer will give you many options. Here again, get to a bookstore and pick out what appears right for you and try to duplicate it. If you go with a good Designer/typesetter, she will help you make this decision.

■ **Letter size.** Again, whom are you writing the book for? Bigger letters work better for the very young or old.

■ **Letter design.** Generally speaking, the simpler the style, the better. If you are writing a book about the olden days, you may want fancy letters but frankly, it is far easier to get a chain store buyer to select your book if it isn't difficult to read the words!

■ **Words per line.** The size of your letters and the dimensions of your book will help you make this decision. Just remember that the more material you put on a line the less expensive it will be to produce your book. Generally speaking, if you use 62 characters a line with, for example, 10 words per line, this will help you make an accurate count. Of course if you are writing to scholars, your average word may have more

letters so that will need an adjustment. Remember that when counting words per line, you will need to also count punctuation and spaces between words as characters.

■ **Lines per page.** Again, how big is your book? If it is nine inches vertically, than you can generally figure on 36 lines per page being about right. Don't forget to leave space between topics though when counting. Also leave "white space" at the top of each chapter's start too!

Collectively, most of the previous few items are normally referred to as "Font" or "Typestyle," and for proper selection, your designer/typesetter will be invaluable. She/he will help you determine what the answers to these questions will be. Without someone helping, even if you have professional page layout software, you are on your own!

■ **Book binding.** The name most used in the past for the typical bookstore book is "Perfect." "Perfect," maybe, because this kind of binding really fits most needs, and stands up over the test of time. I don't recommend any of the other styles, such as stapled, "lay flat," cloth, or spiral wire. Some printers have added an alternative to perfect binding called "adhesive paper cover with hinge score." This is basically single pages that are glued in place, then glued to the cover. This type of binding doesn't follow the 16-page rule.

Select carefully here because if you write one book, anticipating another to follow later, it will be tough to get buyers to go for #2, no matter how good it's content, if #1 has a cover that comes off!

■ **Cover material.** Many a book cover, no matter how well thought out and attractive, will bend with time. If your book stands up on a shelf but the plastic coating on the otherwise beautiful cover causes it to warp or bend, anticipate very unhappy merchants and book buyers! Select carefully here. Of course, a major part of this selection involves whom you get to print it! Consultation with your printer, with the assistance of your designer, is critical here. You need to know what kind of lamination to select — as in film lam-dull, gloss texture, and the weights of the cover stock, such as 10 pt CIS-12 pt CIS, etc. Be very, very careful here because the cover quality counts, big time!

■ **Cover color.** Regardless of what words and pictures you place on your front and back covers, the actual colors you select for the cover will play a part in determining if the buyer will buy the book. Subliminal, yes, but bookstore browsers are attracted to bright colors! If your books are stacked binding out, like most are, it is even tougher to get someone to pick it out from the others. Certainly the subject matter alone can sell the book if readers know it is available, but for folks who just stumble onto your book, they will pick it up and look at it quicker if they are attracted to it.

If the book is placed face out or better yet, is put on a display table or "end-capped" (put at the end of a container), even better but again, the reader must find it and color attracts attention. Typically, the best colors are red and yellow. (Just think about the bright yellow that the "Dummies" series uses.) Sharp red and or yellow will help you, as will silver and blue. Just use this simple rule of thumb: Bright colors work best!

■ **Number of pages.** Generally speaking, the more pages, the more you have to pay to get the book printed. Of course if the subject material is of such interest that it takes 200+ pages to cover it all, then by all means, go for it! Just remember that the more pages, the more it will cost you. Yes, your ultimate buyer will have to spend more money too because your cover price will need to reflect your higher overall cost. Just remember though that if you are looking to do a page count, your printer counts in a very specific way. They count by sixteen's. When a printing machine runs, it makes pages that involve more than a single little page. They are printed in sheets and then cut.

■ **Paper color and weight.** For whatever it's worth, the paper that this book was printed on is called "60# white offset." Make sure you know what color and weight to pick and don't allow your printer to sell you cheap stock to save money. "House stock" might be fine, but if in doubt, don't buy it because it might not hold up over the test of time.

■ **The Spine.** It must have the book's title printed on it or else few retailers will agree to carry it. They generally want the author's name on it as well and if space is available, the publisher's name too.

## ON-DEMAND PRINTING/PRINT QUANTITY

This is a relatively new process of printing books. Generally, people who want to have a very limited number of books printed select this route. For help in explaining how this works, I turned to Kathleen Marada, of Publishers Graphics in Carol Stream, Illinois for assistance. Earlier, I told you about how the negatives for my first three books were destroyed. Well, it was this company that did reprints for me of them, using copies of the actual books themselves. The following are Ms. Marada's comments:

"On-demand printing and print quantity needed are two relatively new approaches to book manufacturing that have opened new avenues for self-publishers. These processes allow an individual the option of having their books printed and bound without involving a publisher. The processes produce an identical product; however, the differences in the two enable different marketing approaches.

By definition, on-demand printing is the process by which a book is produced after it has been ordered. For example, a consumer goes to a bookstore and requests a title that is not at the store. The store orders the title from the publisher, author, or distributor, and that one book is printed, bound and shipped to the individual. This process is mostly used for books that are at the end of the life cycle, and the option keeps the book from going out of print.

The print quantity needed process follows the same procedures as large print runs; however, the quantity is just smaller. Print quantity needed usually refers to orders that are under 1000 and is most often used with new titles. This process allows an individual to print a small quantity of books and market them in the traditional manner. That is, they are available in bookstores, and online via Internet bookstores and/or the individual's website. Once the initial order is sold, the author can produce additional books in the same manner, or opt for a larger print run if the demand for the book warrants such. The advantage of the print quantity needed process is that it allows the person to test the market with a book that is of equal or superior quality to that of traditional processes, without investing a large amount of money in inventory.

The stepping-stone that brought these processes into play was desktop publishing. Most short run book manufacturers print books using digital equipment and therefore prefer to receive digital files for both the text and covers. Digitally printed text and covers are produced directly from the files provided, so the process eliminates the cost of film and plates that are associated with traditional printers. As with traditional printers, the quality of output depends on the company that you select to print your books. During the past few years, digital equipment manufacturers have dramatically improved the quality of color output, allowing four-color process covers to be affordable in the short run arena. Full flood coverage and a wide array of graphic images can be utilized by an individual to create a cover that in the past could only have been achieved on an offset press.

With the awareness of the processes, individuals who want to self-publish and small publishers who want to produce more titles will find the ability to obtain high quality books and fulfill their desire to see their products in print."

*Kathleen Marada, Vice President*
*Publishers Graphics, Carol Stream, IL*

## SELF-PROMOTION

Well before your book comes out, you need to let the outside world know about it. After all, you have prepared to invest $10,000 or so and would like to have readers standing by, waiting to buy it. In order to accomplish this, if you don't go with an agent, you need to know how to beat your own drum!

Drum beating is very difficult to get listened to if everyone plays ostrich. If they bury their heads in the sand, they will never hear about your work. Therefore, as hunters often do quite illegally, "salt your field." In the world of shotguns, that means that a hunter might bait an open field for a day or two before hunting with food that birds, game, etc. like to eat. And then on the arrival of sunup on Opening Day of the season, *voilá!* There's game out there waiting to get whacked!

Well, that is both cruel and illegal, but "salting" a field is not at all inappropriate and for sure, is something that you really should do!

How to do it? Well, selecting a subject as an example, let's say you are going to write a book about condo rules and regulations. And does that sound boring, or what? However, to owners or potential owners of a condo, you may have "gold" in your mind or partially entered into your word processor. Now, to get people to know that such a book is coming out!

Your market for this book is as broad as your own imagination! Even if such books exist, with the advent of every corner of the globe having a hunk of cement and wood plopped down on it in multiple dwelling occupancy format, your list of potential buyers is quite vast.

And again, this is only an example. We ask you to adapt it for the specialty that you are writing about. For every subject, there are lots of people interested in it. Just spend some time learning how to get a list of places to tell about your book.

For your hypothetical condo book, if regional or universal in scope, write to state real estate licensing departments to get a full list of all licensees. More simply, just "let your fingers do the walking," as Ma Bell used to say. Write to every realtor you can find in the book! Write to every condo management association. And also write to every condo association themselves too. Don't stop — send a letter to the real estate section of every newspaper you can get addresses for.

Tell these people that you are writing a book about Condo

rules and I bet readers will run, not walk, to look into buying a copy. We who have owned condos (that probably includes as many as half of you readers too) sometimes feel that our board runs itself like a police state and to have knowledge about this subject may be something they all want to read about. (Hey, maybe I'll write such a book once I get done with "So You Want To Write A Book!")

Seriously, banging that drum before you publish your book is extremely important, and your list of places to outreach to is, again, up to your own imagination.

If the book is about tennis, write to every tennis club you can find. Ask them to tell their members about it, and while you are at it, find out if they would like to sell the book! Chances are good that they will. They all sell shirts, rackets, balls, etc., why not books?

Self-promotion includes writing to all the newspapers, radio and television stations, etc. Lists of them can easily be found in your local library if the book is regional, but if not, with some extra time, you can get lists in other ways too. There are many companies that will sell you pre-printed gummed label lists in every conceivable specialty. Look them up too in your library!

If you are already established as a writer on the subject of your book, you have a waiting audience, but if you don't write a column now, why not start, quickly?

Offer your services free of charge to every weekly newspaper you can find out about. Don't stop with those that charge for the paper either. The TV books and other magazines that are mailed out free of charge all have an editor who might very well like to print a story about what is going on in a particular subject in their reading area. Some of these "freebies" are chain in scope too, so contacting one editor might get your work into a number of newspapers.

If you live in a condo development that has a newsletter, offer to write an article or two about the subject that your book will cover. Even if you think it may be of no interest to the newsletter's editor, you might be surprised to have them welcome your offer with open arms. Here too, if the newsletter involves a managing agent that represents a series of associations, you may get your articles into five or six such association newsletters. Every occupant will read your story and be a potential book buyer.

If you already are in print, great, but it is not too tough to arrange for this if you price your services right. The best price is FREE. If your material is good, many an editor will jump to print a piece on an item of interest to his/her readers. What you want in exchange is simple, really. You want publicity for your book — the book that is about to come out, or may already have been published.

If you write an article for a sports magazine that specializes in bowling, and your book is about bowling, imagine how many people will buy your book as a result.

When you offer your services to such editors, make absolutely clear that they will help you promote the book. Mere mention may not be sufficient. Ask for (well, try to demand politely) that they print your name, address, telephone number, book title, and price for you too. If you have a website, ask them to print that as well. Leave nothing out if you get enough space — tell readers about tax, if any, shipping and handling charges, etc. (I recommend saying "NO shipping and handling charges" to encourage readers to buy your book.)

Get as much free space in exchange for your free story as you can, and plead with the editor to run your ad on the same page that your article appears. Advance orders will surely follow if your articles are good! Make sure you refer to your book every now and then in your articles as well. This will increase sales.

Clearly, you stand a very good chance at getting interest in your book if you are already in print about the subject matter. If you write a weekly column about bird watching, you are "established" and frequent mention that you have a book coming out about it will have interested readers anxiously awaiting the book itself.

While you are accomplishing a list of ready readers this way, you will also find out that storeowners or managers, as well as librarians, might also be reading your columns, and thus finding out about your book. Volume sales may result this way.

Be sure to write to other writers who have columns that involve your subject matter. When I wrote my third book about fishing, a fellow fishing columnist who I had never met somehow or another found out about it, got a copy, and wrote quite favorably about it in one of his columns. I discovered this in the strangest of ways. I got a single order from a library that is in the town that his paper gets published. Before I could think about it, another nearby library ordered a copy, and then I called both places and was told what I just told you. Using this, I got a list of all the libraries in my state and, making it brief, that book is now in over 130 libraries in New Jersey. Of equal importance, the managing editor of Rutgers University Press found out about that book and bought a copy at a bookstore and hired me later to write two books for them!

You never know how much of a bang for your buck you can get by writing to other people who write about your basic subject matter. Most of these scribes will be happy to help you, in particular, if the book is good!

In the next chapter we talk about publicity, via the use of an agent/publicist. Frankly, while you may know how to get material out to a handful of fellow writers, these people have limitless resources and knowledge so if you have some extra money budgeted, get an agent and watch just how much outreach will be done for you.

Once the book actually comes out, write to every TV and radio station, plus all the newspapers and magazines you can find, but first try to find out who the right person is. A letter "To whom it may concern" will probably wind up in the circular file. Spend a lot of time on the telephone asking who the book reviewer is and send it to her/him!

"Review copies" are generally a cheap version of your book. If you have never seen one, walk in to your local bookstore and ask the manager to show you one. Chances are good to excellent that it was never opened! A review copy usually is printed with a dull blue color cover, on cheap paper, and almost dares folks to open it. Most will not, and such copies are, in my opinion, a waste of time and money, used incorrectly as a way to tell people about your book while trying to save money too. Frankly, the only review copy that you have a good chance at being looked at is a copy of the book itself. Remember what we said earlier? You can't tell a book by its cover but it sure helps! A nice cover will get the reviewer to at least think about it!

# PUBLICITY

Assuming a few things, like your book will not only make an interesting read but that it will be well received, leaves the matter of getting people to know about it.

The best way to do this would be via an agent, also known as publicist, someone who is paid to gather as much free publicity as possible for you. Of course "free" is not quite accurate, because you have to pay the agent to get readers to know about the book. Some agents require an advance fee as well as a percentage of sales, and each such representative will require you to go into contract, to make certain that you don't try to break your agreement later on. In case you do go with an agent, it would be worth your while to hire an attorney to assist in drawing up the contract, or if the agency uses its own form, at least to review it for you.

It is not fair to cheat someone out of a well-deserved fee. However, your contract should clearly spell out what you are getting for your money and or percentage of sales, so that you will have grounds in the event the agent doesn't perform to the letter of the agreement.

These agents will take care of publicity for you and if you are not capable of handling such matters for yourself, I strongly urge you to get one. Without doubt, no one can sell your book for you better than you (well, maybe Oprah or Imus can), but an agent will do it for you if you are not inclined to become aggressive about it.

A list of such agents can be obtained from *Literary Market Place* but just as an example, here's a few that I found listed in "The Self-Publishing Manual" and talked to personally.

- Alan Caruba — Maplewood, NJ — 1-973-763-6392

- Kate Bandos — Ada, MI — 1-616-676-0758

- Irwin Zucker — Hollywood, CA — 1-323-461-3921

- Sherri Rosen — Milltown, NJ — 1-732-448-9441

All four told me that they handle lots of non-fiction self-publishers, with a wide variety of services offered.

On the other hand, if you think that you have a flair for sales, you might want to try it for yourself. Unless you are already well known in your field though, consider it close to impossible to break through without professional assistance. Use the information in the previous chapter as your guide to see if you have a shot at self-promotion.

CHAPTER SIX

# Insurance

And now for a subject that puts most people quickly to sleep. "Yawn," you say? Well, honestly, it really is a dreadfully dreary topic but in spite of all that, I suggest you read these words very carefully to avoid some extreme problems that might occur in the future.

There are lots of ways to "buy" insurance, or to "get" it. Let's start with one that I hope you will never need.

■ **Plagiarism Insurance.** If you set out to steal something from someone else with clear intent, most policies that protect the policyholder from suit brought on behalf of writers for such acts are not really well covered. You see, it is against public policy to cover you for a crime!

If you write a book that simply "comes to you" and it really is based on another work, or worse, actually contains written words that were taken without crediting the author by accident, you can be sued and you might very well lose. The more popular the "harmed," the worse you can be whacked! If you publish a book of what you call your own original songs and one or two were close variations of someone else's work, again, watch your back.

Before you put your words to paper, or at least before they get printed, try to assure yourself that you have not remembered something that someone else wrote first. Seek coverage against plagiarism lawsuits if you wish, but make sure you understand the fine print to see what you really are covered for.

By the way, this policy often can cover you too for suits involving libel or defamation of character. If your statements are so blatantly false though, your carrier might deny responsibility to protect you. In any event, you may find that the premium may be exorbitant!

■ **Cargo/Transit Insurance.** This is, or at least should be, carried by the company you hired to print your book. If they do their own trucking, they carry, or should carry, "cargo" insurance to cover them if a shipment is lost, stolen, damaged by weather or collision, or burned up. If they don't do their own trucking but instead hire contract carriers, hope that they carry "transit" insurance, just in case their trucker doesn't have the best form of "cargo" insurance.

Okay, take a few aspirins for your headache now and think about it. The books are not really "yours" yet, if your contract says so, even though you probably paid at least ¾ of the price by now. However, you don't want to get stuck in the middle of a fight between your printer and their trucker or insurance carrier. Here again is a very good reason to pick your printer with extreme care. When interviewing them, make sure, in writing, that they have insurance. Of course, insurance alone doesn't do it. "Acts of God" like weather may not be covered. If the truck goes up in smoke when smashed by lightning or flipped over in a hurricane, your books may become material for the garbage dump, and the damage may not be covered!

Make sure your printer will reprint quickly if a load is destroyed rather than wait for their claim to be settled before going to the presses again. Get this in writing!

■ **Premises Insurance.** Most self-publishers keep inventory in their home, even once they get into multiple printings. Clearly, if you can afford to do so, put your stock into a fire-proof or at least a brick structure, but if you are going to keep it in your basement or garage, watch out!

You can protect the books from water damage by putting them on skids or pallets, but you still had better protect them with an insurance policy.

Oh, you already carry insurance, you say? Yes, your home-owner's policy will cover you for damage to the house and its contents but the fine print clearly says that "business property" isn't covered — at all! Homeowner's policies can be endorsed to protect a professional like a doctor, lawyer, etc., but we writers simply aren't in that league! Your books are NOT insured!

A very fine wholesaler who I did business with in Pennsylvania had a total loss, caused by fire, at his premises and went out of business. I really am not certain but my educated guess is that he didn't have any business insurance coverage.

Buy a business insurance policy even before your books get delivered. Call your own agent and ask if they have expertise in such matters. Many are well skilled in personal insurance, e.g. life, car, house, but rarely are called in to handle busi-nesses. Therefore, get someone who knows this subject well. If your own agent isn't highly skilled in these matters she/he should be able to send you to an expert.

The commonly used name for the kind of policy you want is a "BOP," or Business Owners Policy. By any name, it covers you for loss of or damage to your inventory. It also will cover you if your accountant declared the room you do your writing in "business use." If that room and its computer, desk, filing cabinet, etc., was purchased in the business name you use, or designated as "business," your homeowners' policy probably won't cover you for damage to the contents of that room!

The "BOP" should cover you for the actual replacement value of everything owned by the "business." Your computer may be a few years old and better ones were manufactured

*"Get them up on skids ... just in case."*

since, but you still want dollars to replace it. "Actual Cash Value" is a term used to allow an insurer to depreciate your claim and as with a used car, you may only get half of the money needed to replace it unless the policy provides "replacement" coverage.

Forgetting the stuff in your office, let's go to the books now. When you buy your policy, anticipate what your need will be and make sure to adjust later. For example, if you write a book and it was followed by another and again another, don't forget to increase your limit of protection if inventory starts to pile up.

You may have 1,500 of the original 3,000 books left from your first issue, and take delivery of another book that involved a print run of 5,000 copies. Presuming a fire destroys all, if the first book cost you an average of $2 each, you probably won't be able to replace the damage at that rate because your cost savings based on large print runs will be gone. Ditto the 5,000 book run. If you paid $1.50 per book to the printer and half the books are totaled, the unit cost will be higher to reprint the missing 2,500.

As discussed earlier, the disk that you have stuck away in a drawer for safety is probably the biggest risk you have to protect. Even if you have duplicated the disk, it may be in another room. If that little piece of very flammable plastic goes up in smoke, your book will go with it. Make sure that another full copy of your original disk exists in another building somewhere safe. Your mother's home, maybe your son's, would be a cheap way to do it, but please, even if you backed up the book several times in your computer and have a few copies of it on disk in the house, that fire will clobber you. Your insurance policy may cover you for the time and effort needed to recreate the book, but here "Self-Insurance" in the form of proper and complete duplication is better yet. Even if you have a load of books in stores to retype from, how about the photos and artwork?

The lesson here is to buy sufficient insurance and know that, if your policy covers "Replacement Cost," that will be based on what you have to pay to "replace" the books.

Most "BOP's" also cover loss of earnings, sometimes called "Business Interruption" insurance, and this can be very valuable protection indeed. While the direct damage to your inventory can be protected against, what about the income you lost as a result of the incident? Loss of earnings coverage should be included in your policy. If it is not automatically included, make sure to buy some.

Your "BOP" may also be endorsed to cover you for loss of or damage to your accounts receivable records. Of course, if you duplicate your records in another building and update them often, this won't be as important (but let's face it, most of us won't do that). Therefore, make sure your policy protects you for the amount of money you will lose if your billing records are destroyed by a disaster.

And "Valuable Papers" coverage too might be another item of protection to add. This covers the cost of replacing such "valuable papers" that might be lost or destroyed by a covered claim like fire, explosion, etc.

Another feature of your policy may involve protection for loss of or damage to your inventory if you are making a large delivery yourself via vehicle. Whether you are driving to the post office or UPS — maybe to the wholesaler who ordered five cartons — make sure your policy covers you for such an incident. Your car insurance will not cover you for the destruction of your books, no matter what the cause (again, "Business Property" exclusion, remember?)

Most policies also protect you against lawsuits brought by people who claim to have been injured in one way or another by your "company." If a trucker is making a delivery of books to you and is injured, his employer's worker's compensation policy will cover them for the injury, but the guy may elect to sue you too. Your homeowner's policy may not cover you, based on the same "Business Exclusion" we discussed above.

In addition, if you do signings, attend book shows, etc., you may be subject to suit if you somehow or another are accused of causing injury. Then too, "insurance consultants" are in the business of telling their corporate clients to not do any business with anyone unless they carry adequate liability insurance. While this seems silly at first, if you want to get your books directly into any of the big chain stores, you had better carry at least $1,000,000 of liability insurance. This will normally be found within your "BOP." And the very same consultant will probably want all vendors (that's what they will call you, even if you don't push a cart) to carry "Product Liability" insurance. Foolish at first glance, this will cover you if someone gets a paper cut from your book. After having spent 41 years in the business of insuring businesses, I cannot really think of any other legitimate reason for such a demand but instead of fighting, buy the protection. It usually is a throw-in within your little package policy anyway.

Generally, the liability part of your policy might also protect you against suits brought by people who accuse you of libel or defamation of character. Some "tell-all" books certainly do point accusing fingers, and as a result, an accusation that blames you for incorrect and damaging written words could be the result, and might be covered too.

So, wake up now, we are nearly done with the chapter about insurance. There is really only one thing left.

■ **Shipping Insurance.** While Dan Poynter in his superb book, "The Self-Publishing Manual," advises against buying protection for loss of individual books that you are sending, I disagree to a point.

Once upon a time we used to sell what was called "Parcel Post" insurance. The meaning was that a business would buy coverage for such losses. Agency-sold policies were a major annoyance to everyone and we found that insurance purchased directly from the post office was probably best.

Way back when, the cost for this protection was as little as 25 cents per $100 of value. A $500 shipment would only cost $1.25, but things have changed. Post office insurance may cost as much as $2 per $100 and the rate drops based on higher values. However, if you lose a box of books, the insurance suddenly seems to be a good idea.

I personally buy insurance on most full carton shipments but leave the decision up to you. Clearly, don't do this if you are sending a book or two to a mail order purchaser. So what if you lose the full price? Just send her one or two more! You still make a profit.

If you have billed a full box of 80 books at, for example, $9 each but your cost was only $2 apiece, you still might want to insure it at 80 x $9 or $720 instead of at 80 x $2 or $160. If the box disappears and your sale involved a need to be on time, your customer may not want you to re-ship. If they will wait, you may only want to buy the $160 coverage limit, or maybe a little more because you will have to pay for shipping and insurance twice. In such a case I generally buy at a higher limit than my cost per book. For this situation I would buy $250 of insurance.

The better-known over-the-road shippers like UPS and Federal Express normally provide coverage to you as part of the charge they collect for shipping. However, here the fine print clicks in. It will probably say that their responsibility to you is limited to not more than $100 or so. And you will probably have to sign something that says so, even if you don't know it. The protection afforded is nearly always limited in scope to a dollar amount. So if you do elect to send a box or two or more via such companies, you may want to buy separate additional coverage from them, OR, carry your own Transit Insurance if you get big enough.

■ **Off-Premises Coverage.** You may need to protect inventory while elsewhere. Make sure your policy covers you for inventory in a storage building or out on consignment. Biblio, Unique, and Quality, and others may say that they are not responsible for your stuff, therefore buy off-premises protection!

Before you get into the next subject, you will have to decide what is best for you. Dan Poynter, the Guru of self-publishers, wrote an article for *WD* in the April 2002 edition, talking about self-publishing, in which he said: "Many non-fiction writers look for an agent or a publisher when they're ready to go to press. But self-publishing beforehand can give you an edge." The man is talking about money, plain and simple, and of course, he is dead on! Later, he continues, "In self-publishing, you invest the money, but you do not have to share the net. You get it all!"

This to the side, you may still want to consider a middle ground of sorts — not self-publishing, not the "Vanity Press" route. And not trying to deal with the countless rejection slips that usually come from the conventional publishing houses, nor the need to lay out $10,000 or so, I call it... *(See next chapter.)*

# CHAPTER SEVEN

# An Alternative To Self-Publishing
## The University Press

We have spent lots of time talking about the concept of self-publishing, and I've told you why you really may be taking too much of a risk going through the vanity or subsidy press method. The alternative is the use of a "university press."

To avoid spending countless hours going after a publisher and enduring the pile of pink slips and still more rejections, an alternative is available that may produce better results. True, university presses are indeed real "publishers," but still you may find them better to deal with than the more traditional publishing houses.

In particular, if the book you want to write is a non-fiction work, and is either based on a scholarly subject or perhaps is regional in scope, many state universities and lots of other colleges actually have subsidiaries that independently act as publishing companies.

Therefore, we have yet one more reason for your book to be a "local" one, especially if you feel that sufficient interest exists in your state or region on the subject.

Let's face it. Self-publishing is far from a cheap matter. If you don't have the money set aside to publish a book and also have some leftover cash to help you publicize it, self-publishing may be a very bad idea indeed. The worst thing I can think of is to write a great book and get stuck with it because no one will print it and you cannot afford to do it yourself.

Your own personal "15 minutes of fame" can easily be achieved when a conventional publishing company buys your book, yes, IF you can get someone to accept your manuscript. Equally, if you self-publish you will at least be able to show the book to friends for the purpose of bragging about your skill, but that will have cost you big bucks.

I direct you to a fine book that will tell you which universities actually do own subsidiary presses. Two of my books were published by such an institution (Rutgers University Press), and I value the experiences highly.

The book I refer to is entitled "The Association of American University Presses" and it comes out every year. The 2001-2002 directory that I purchased provides "information on 121 scholarly presses in the United States, Canada, and overseas." The modest outlay of cash for the book was well worth spending, if only for me to be able to provide details for you.

If your decision to self-publish is not rock solid and you would like to think of an alternative, this is the book for you.

The directory publishes all the names and addresses of every such university press, giving telephone and fax numbers for each, and also allows you to see what kind of written material they accept for publishing. Again, I found the book most useful, but to help you further, I wrote separate letters and faxed them to nearly 50 of the presses to see if they in fact actually do publish "books." You see, many print "papers" on important subject matters, but not necessarily the kind of "book" you may have in mind.

If you are writing a non-fiction regional book, on most any subject, your local college may be the answer. Many will only print books on scholarly subjects, but quite a few will also accept books that touch on matters of interest in their own state.

There are many reasons to think about a university press, but to cite a few examples, right out of the directory:

1. "University presses encourage and refine the work of younger scholars through publication of the first books that establish credentials and develop authorial experience."

2. "University presses help connect the university to the surrounding community by publishing books of local interest and hosting events for local authors."

3. "University presses give voice to minority cultures and perspectives through pioneering publication programs in ethnic, racial, and sexual studies."

4. "University presses help to preserve the distinctiveness of local cultures through publication of works on the states and regions where they are based."

And there are lots of other reasons to go this way too.

A university press can go into contract with you in the same manner as a conventional publisher. For manuscripts that they accept, a modest fee is usually paid and your contract will say that the school will also pay you a fee for books actually sold and paid for. In return, you may be required to give up most of if not all rights to your book forever, and agree to attend signings when possible.

Getting your work published by a university press can take quite a while, as much as a year or more after you go into contract. Although you can write the book in a month or two, the school has lots more to deal with than just your single manuscript. A conventional publishing house may take even longer unless the material is timely in scope, such as with the World Trade Center attack. You can publish your own book in a fraction of the time, but you will also have to lay out the dollars to do so. And yes, you will make far more money self-publishing, if the book sells, but a university press doesn't cost you any money at all!

Seek schools that are near where you live first and then expand your horizons. You have a far better shot at getting a university press in your own region to accept your book, especially if it is about your area.

Buy the AAUP Directory, please, but for a very brief list of these organizations, in alphabetical order by state, here's my own list. If there are two or more presses in a state, the list will show them alphabetically within that state. It may not be completely accurate, but I hope it helps. I have listed the schools that print at least 10 books yearly. It may contain an error or two and for that, I apologize, but the idea here is to give you an option that varies from the basic one: self-publishing.

Asterisks note the schools that clearly do publish "books." The others PROBABLY publish books too.

The telephone number is shown first and then the fax number. If the three digits that follow the area code are the same for the telephone and fax numbers, they will not be repeated, but if those three numbers differ sometimes, the full number will be listed.

| State | Name of University Press | Phone/FaxNumber |
|-------|--------------------------|-----------------|
| AK | University of Arkansas | 501-575-3246/6044 |
| AZ | University of Arizona | 520-621-1441/8899 |
| CA | University of California | 510-642-4247 643-7127 |
|  | Stanford* | 650-723-9434 725-3457 |
| CO | University Press of Colorado | 720-406-8849/3443 |
| CT | Wesleyan* | 860-685-2420/2421 |
|  | Yale* | 203-432-0960/0948 |
| DC | Georgetown | 202-687-5889/6340 |
| FL | University Press of Florida | 352-392-1351/7302 |
| GA | University of Georgia* | 706-369-6130/6131 |
|  | Mercer University Press | 478-301-2880/2264 |

*This university press definitely publishes books.*

| State | Name of University Press | Phone/FaxNumber |
|-------|--------------------------|-----------------|
| HI | University of Hawaii* | 808-956-8257 988-6052 |
| IA | University of Iowa* | 319-335-2000/2055 |
| IL | University of Chicago* | 773-702-7700/2705 |
|  | University of Illinois* | 217-333-0950 244-8082 |
|  | Northern Illinois | 815-753-1826/1845 |
|  | Northwestern* | 847-491-5313/8150 |
|  | Southern Illinois* | 618-453-2281/1221 |
| IN | Indiana University Press | 812-855-8817/8507 |
|  | Notre Dame* | 219-631-6346/8148 |
|  | Purdue* | 765-494-2038 496-2442 |
| KS | University Press of Kansas | 785-864-4154/4586 |
| KT | University Press of Kentucky* | 859-257-4249 323-1873 |
| LA | Louisiana State* | 225-578-6294/6461 |
| MA | Harvard* | 617-495-2600/5898 |
|  | University of Massachusetts* | 413-545-2217/1226 |
|  | MIT* | 617-253-5646 258-6779 |
|  | Northeastern* | 617-373-5480/5483 |
| MD | Johns Hopkins* | 410-516-6900/6998 |
| MI | University of Michigan* | 734-764-4388 615-1540 |
|  | Michigan State* | 517-355-9543 353-6766 |
|  | Wayne State* | 313-577-4600/6131 |
| MN | University of Minnesota | 612-627-1970/1980 |
| MO | University of Missouri* | 573-882-7641 884-4498 |
| MS | University Press of Mississippi | 601-432-6205/6217 |
| NC | Duke* | 919-687-3600 688-4574 |
|  | University of North Carolina | 919-966-3561/3829 |
| NE | University of Nebraska* | 402-472-3581/0308 |

*This university press definitely publishes books.*

| State | Name of University Press | Phone/FaxNumber |
| --- | --- | --- |
| NH | University Press of New England* | .603-643-7100/7117 |
| NJ | Princeton* . . . . . . . . . . . . . . . . . . | .609-258-4900/6305 |
| | Rutgers* . . . . . . . . . . . . . . . . . . | .732-445-7762/7039 |
| NM | University of New Mexico* . . . . . . | .505-277-2346/9270 |
| NV | University of Nevada* . . . . . . . . . . | .775-784-6573/6200 |
| NY | Columbia* . . . . . . . . . . . . . . . . . . | .212-459-0600/3677 |
| | Fordham . . . . . . . . . . . . . . . . . . | .718-817-4780/4785 |
| | NYU . . . . . . . . . . . . . . . . . . . . | .212-998-2575 995-3833 |
| | State University of New York* . . . | .518-472-5000/5038 |
| | Syracuse* . . . . . . . . . . . . . . . . . . | .315-443-5534/5545 |
| OH | Kent State . . . . . . . . . . . . . . . . . . | .330-672-7913/3104 |
| | Ohio . . . . . . . . . . . . . . . . . . . . . | .740-593-1155/4536 |
| | Ohio State* . . . . . . . . . . . . . . . . | .614-292-6930/2065 |
| OK | University of Oklahoma* . . . . . . | .405-325-2000/4000 |
| OR | Oregon State* . . . . . . . . . . . . . . | .541-737-3166/3170 |
| PA | Carnegie Mellon* . . . . . . . . . . | .412-268-2861 fax same # |
| | University of Pennsylvania* . . . . . | .215-898-6261/0404 |
| | Penn State* . . . . . . . . . . . . . . | .814-865-1327 863-1408 |
| | Temple* . . . . . . . . . . . . . . . . . . | .215-204-8787/4719 |
| | University of Pittsburgh . . . . . . . | .412-383-2456/2466 |
| | University of Scranton . . . . . . . . | .570-941-4228/4309 |
| SC | University of South Carolina* . . . | .803-777-5243/0160 |
| TN | University of Tennessee* . . . . . . . | .865-974-3321/3724 |
| TX | University of Texas* . . . . . . . . | .512-471-7233 320-0668 |
| | Texas A&M* . . . . . . . . . . . . . | .979-845-1436 847-8752 |
| | Texas Christian* . . . . . . . . . . . . | .817-257-7822/5075 |
| | Texas Tech.* . . . . . . . . . . . . . . | .806-742-2982/2979 |

* This university press definitely publishes books.

| State | Name of University Press | Phone/FaxNumber |
|-------|--------------------------|-----------------|
| UT | University of Utah . . . . . . . . . . . . .801-581-6771/3365 |
|    | Utah State* . . . . . . . . . . . . . . . . .435-797-1362/0313 |
| VA | University Press of Virginia* . .804-924-3468 982-2655 |
| WA | University of Washington* . . . . . .206-543-4050/3932 |
|    | Washington State . . . . . . . . . . . . .509-335-3518/8568 |
| WI | Marquette . . . . . . . . . . . . . . . . . .414-288-7813/3300 |
|    | University of Wisconsin* . . . . . . . .608-263-1110/1132 |

*This university press definitely publishes books.*

With apologies to those universities that do publish books that I did not credit with asterisks before and after their names, again, my regrets. Unfortunately, as wonderful as the AAUP book was, I still couldn't clearly see which do and don't print books.

If you are going to write about garage sales in New Mexico, you may not want to submit your idea to The University of South Carolina, of course. So use your own common sense before you select a school to offer your book to. It isn't fair to bother them with material that simply makes no sense at all. But once again, if you find a school in this list that is in your own state, or is right next door to the area that you want to write about, go for it!

By the way, the AAUP book also has names and addresses of a variety of foreign university presses, and in particular, quite a few in Canada. So if your book will be about Canada or at least an area close by, think about contacting those universities also. Once again, you need the book for this! The Directory also shows certain religious presses and specialty ones like The American Chemical Society, Getty Publications, National Gallery of Art, etc.

# CHAPTER EIGHT

# Selling Your Book

## "Getting Someone To Buy The Doggone Thing!"

### SELLING ORDER

Most people in sales find "face-to-face" very difficult, but let's go over what I call "Selling Order" and provide you with a very unofficial rating system for each kind. We will omit anything to do with a computer for now though.

■ **Face-to-face.** Toughest to do by far, but if you can find a buyer and talk directly to them, you stand the best chance of making a sale. In fact, whether it is a store or library, if you have any self-confidence at all, you might find out that you make a sale to as many as 75% of them!

■ **Telephone sales.** We will spend much more time on this later in the telemarketing section but for now, please understand that if you do get a buyer on the telephone, and are good at it, you will wind up with as many as 50% of all calls resulting in a sale!

■ **First class mailings.** This one is way down in the list. The prettiest of all presentations might produce a 5-10% return.

■ **Cheap mailings.** Last also least is cheap mailings, and it is the format used by most people who are trying to make a sale. Face it, if you are like me, when you get junk mail you throw it away. Of course, if you are also like me, you might first look inside for a postage free return envelope and then you mail back the empty return envelope to make them pay the postage! Unless you are after exercise, don't waste your money trying to save money this way. If lucky, you might get a 2-3% return, but more likely, less than that!

## TOUGH TIMES

When times are tough, especially when a recession is present, it becomes all that more difficult to get buyers to buy. However, readers often find the money when they need to escape, or to learn, and your book could be just what the doctor ordered. You can bet that the book store chain buyers will be even more careful in selecting what to buy when money is short, but don't let hard times stop you from writing. Once your book is out, just realize that you will have to work even harder to get people to buy it.

In writing about how to deal with recessions in the April 2002 issue of WD, Jeffery D. Zbar wrote: "It takes stamina and a positive outlook to ensure the enterprise emerges stronger when the storm has cleared." Therefore, don't let anything stand in your way, just deal with whatever appears. Good or bad times, unless you are quite famous, buyers will not get in line to buy your book until they know it exists, so locate the right people.

Your best market would be the chain stores, of course, but how do you get into them? More books are submitted to bookstore buyers than one could possibly imagine. And clearly, many more are never opened or at least given serious consideration, because time doesn't permit it!

In order to get a book buyer to consider ordering your book, from you, or from a wholesaler, there must be sufficient

| WRITER'S CALENDAR | | | | | | |
|---|---|---|---|---|---|---|
| FRIDAY | FRIDAY | FRIDAY | FRIDAY | FRIDAY | FRIDAY | FRIDAY |
| 13 | 13 | 13 | 13 | 13 | 13 | 13 |
| 13 | 13 | 13 | 13 | 13 | 13 | 13 |
| 13 | 13 | 13 | 13 | 13 | 13 | 13 |
| 13 | 13 | 13 | 13 | 13 | 13 | 13 |
| 13 | 13 | 13 | | | | |

interest in the subject and content. That is where an agent or publicist comes in, but the problem is that most of us cannot afford such a luxury. Furthermore, no good publicist or agent will take on your book unless you can convince them that there is value involved.

No, not a direct payment to these folks. That may work in the short run but truly, unless the agent feels that your book is a good one and that a market exists for it, they really cannot do much to help you out. Your agent may be able to beat your drum quite loudly, but unless folks hear it, the noise will fall on deaf ears.

Therefore, by yourself or with a representative, you have to do something to get buyers to know that you are out there.

## WHEN TO SELL THE BOOK

When? Always, that's when. That said, there really are better times and days to try to sell your book. The art of selling involves "when" more then anything else. In our telemarketing section, we go into this in more detail. Suffice it to say that you should never, never, try to push a buyer when they are really too busy to be pushed. Just use this as your basic theme and you will have a leg up towards selling success.

## IN THE SELLING ZONE

Heading back to *WD*, in the February 2000 issue, Susan K. Perry discusses something she calls "Go With The Flow," as it relates to writing. She advises readers that you'll know that you are "In the Flow" when time flies by quickly and favorably. One can easily say that this works just as well when you are trying to sell as when you are trying to write.

Use Ms. Perry's thoughts when you write your book, but also let this idea work to help motivate you with selling as well. You will find that the more calls you make, the better your chances are of scoring a sale. You will then find that you forget about the last five librarians that you called who didn't buy and instead, get quite a charge from the order from #6, even if it is for just one book.

Ms. Perry suggests that ballplayers use the term "being in the zone," when they seem to effortlessly succeed at bat or in the field. Once you are really into it, time will stand still. You will find that you are not hungry, nor thirsty, and even that the porcelain facility doesn't beckon. Sell for all you are worth now, because you will find that you're whole involvement will get even easier. Your words will come out better, as will your approach to sales.

"Be Persistent," wrote Laura Kaminker in the *WD* January 2000 issue. She tells us that she learned this key lesson as a magazine freelancer in connection with trying to get an editor to buy her article, but being aggressive works in connection with book selling just as well.

Well, this book shouts that out to you, big time — BE PERSISTENT! If you really think that you have hit the nail on the head with your book, whatever you have written about, be persistent and show confidence in your sales approaches. After all, if you have convinced yourself, it will be easier to convince buyers too.

## THE TO-TO-TO-TO'S OF SELLING

In order to sell your literary work, you have to learn about all of the to-to's that are out there. In no particular order, they are: Whom TO, How TO, When TO, and Where TO. We just talked about the When To, let's now talk about the Whom To.

## WHOM TO SELL TO

Yes, chain stores, but how do you get into them? Just about every store of any size sets up a maze that shields its buyers from unsolicited material. Every human who has something to sell thinks that it is the ultimate and clearly, it belongs on shelves clear across the land. But if you don't have a good agent who knows the "To-To's," you will have to get it done yourself. Therein lies one of the better kept secrets of self-publishing. The thrill of success, a/k/a the ego trip. Hey, people are buying YOUR book? Money aside, that makes you feel great!

So, since the book chains sell more books then just about every other method known, here's a list of the bigger ones now, as well as a list of the book wholesalers who have wonderful contacts with these various booksellers. Remember that the big guys really will not want to buy anything directly from you because that causes far too much paperwork for them.

For every new book, most stores have to create what is called an "SKU" (stock keeping unit), and in order to keep up with inventory, many use what is referred to as an "E-3" system. This helps them track via computer the number of pieces they have remaining in stock. The downside is that one nasty, bent or dirty book could be on the shelf that no one will ever buy and since "the computer says we still have inventory," re-orders may never come! These problems aside, here we go with the two groupings, with firm name, city, plus telephone and fax number, if available:

### Book Store Chains

■ **Barnes & Noble, Inc.,** NYC, NY
1-212-633-3300 fax 1-212-675-0413

■ **Borders Books And Music,** Ann Arbor, MI
1-734-477-1100*

■ **Waldenbooks®,** Ann Arbor, MI
1-734-477-1100*

*Note: Borders and Walden are part of one company, but each has its own buyers who make independent decisions. Therefore, if you find someone at Walden who wants your book, you will then have to seek out the buyer at Borders, but it sure couldn't hurt to let that buyer know that their counterpart wants that book also!*

You may find interest with one of the big chains; however, more than likely they will tell you they only buy from wholesalers. Of course "Manager Buy" programs allow lots of individual store managers to order your book directly from you, especially in connection with regional subjects or book signings, but to sell large numbers, you really need a good wholesaler. Some of them are:

### Book Wholesalers

■ **Baker & Taylor,** Momence, IL
1-815-472-2444 fax 1-800-411-8433

■ **Bookazine, Inc. ,** Bayonne, NJ
1-800-221-8112 or 1-201-339-7777
fax 1-201-339-7778

■ **Ingram Book Company,** LaVergne, TN*
1-800-937-8100 or 1-615-793-5000

■ **Washington Book Distributors,** Alexandria, VA
   1-703-212-9113 fax 1-703-212-9114

*\*A new kid has recently appeared on the block who may be quite
good for new self-publishers. In 2002, Ingram wrote to many of their
smaller publishers and said that National Book Network, a huge
distributor, created an entity specifically geared to assist smaller
publishers. That firm is called Biblio Distribution. Presuming that
Biblio wants to try to sell your book, they also provide sales assistance.
Your net income per book will be less this way, but if you aren't good
at selling, this may be the best place for you to go.*

   *To reach Biblio, contact them in Lanham, MD at 1-301-459-
3366 or by fax 1-301-459-1705. Tell them you would like to sell your
book(s) through them, and they will try to help you get started.*

There are many other wholesalers that you can find listed in
"The Self-Publishing Manual," but since I have sold books to
all four of the above firms, AND because they have paid for
them as well, I offer you a first-hand list.

Two other firms specialize in selling books to libraries. In
fact, their salesmen are trained to carry a variety of book
covers with them in their travels. This way, they can show the
cover to acquisition librarians instead of having to drag a
suitcase filled with whole books. Both of these firms have
ordered books from me by the carton. They often require
larger discounts then some of the regular wholesalers. Note
though they usually do things via the devil "consignment"
manner. In English, that means that you send the books and
hope that they sell them, because you won't get paid until the
library pays the wholesaler!

   They are:

### Library Specialists

■ **Quality Books,** Oregon, IL *(The town of Oregon, not state!)*
   1-815-732-4450 fax 815-732-4499

■ **Unique Books,** St. Louis, Mo.
   1-800-533-5446 fax 1-800-916-2455

Many of the conventional book wholesalers also sell to libraries, of course, but the above two are specialists.

It is important to note that while wholesalers put out catalogs that list the titles they have for sale, it is up to you to convince store buyers to order the book from such wholesalers rather than to expect the wholesaler to do the selling for you!

In case you don't know how to reach the two main firms that distribute via the internet, they are:

### Internet Sellers

■ **Amazon.com,** Seattle, WA. Unfortunately, Amazon® really doesn't want to give out their address and telephone number. Although I have given you help with just about every other source I mention in this book, you need to reach out to Amazon via e-mail.

The e-mail address is <advantage@amazon.com>. The website option to sign up and retrieve orders is www.amazon.com/advantage. They are a good company to do business with and I urge you to reach out to them with information about the book you will offer them. They normally want a 55% discount. Once you have hooked up with them, they will e-mail orders to you periodically. The number of orders will only be based on how many folks try to buy your book from them. Having had some success with Amazon, and because, once you are set up with them, they are rather easy to do business with, I suggest that you make the attempt.

Amazon may not want your book, but chances are good that if you submit sufficient data to them, they will at least place a small initial order and make your book available to their countless online customers.

They do not need to be billed. The order they e-mail to you is sufficient for their bookkeeping department to pay from. You will be able to print out their order number, called a

"Shipping ID," and then all you need do is print two copies of the order, wrap the number of books ordered with one copy, and ship them out to the address called for. You will have to also put that Shipping ID# on the outside of your package to assist in identification.

■ **Barnes & Noble Distributors,** New York City — direct mail, not stores (this is their .com entity) — 1-212-414-6000. Once Barnes & Noble gets you set up, orders will follow in connection with how many of their customers order from them via the "net." Their orders may come via fax or mail, but do try to have a fax machine with a dedicated telephone line to make it easier for everyone. The order will ask you to send the number of books sought, with a bill copy. It will have a purchase order number that has to be placed on your bill as well as on the shipping package. Since you are to send an invoice, that envelope also needs to have the PO number shown thereon. The books will have to be sent to their fulfillment warehouse and the bill to their Accounts Payable department.

## WHO ELSE?

The sky's the limit, but for certain, besides chain stores, wholesalers, and internet facilities, there is nothing stopping you but yourself from expanding. Do this by using every means possible to locate buyers.

## "SPEAK UP"

This message was the heading of an article by Patricia L. Fry in the March 2001 issue of *WD*. She offers the notion that in order to sell books, you need exposure. And since you know the most about your book, it is up to you to get out there and talk it up, everywhere! Frankly, if you cannot do this, woe is you. And if you haven't found someone to assist, like a good agent, you might just have to chalk off your experience as a worthwhile effort to get your fifteen minutes of fame, and not much else. Unless you really try to sell your book to any and every possible buying source, you might wind up with a basement full of unsold books. Here again is a place where having a partner who is experienced in sales can be invaluable.

## DIRECT SALES

One way is to set up your own website. Direct sales often produce the greatest pleasure for you. Not only will you usually get the full price, up front, but here again, it's direct ego gratification for you!

To do direct sales best, combine scanned pictures of your book's covers on your website with ease of acquisition. Don't just give your name and address for them to mail you a check, although this is a viable first step. Contact your bank and arrange for credit card purchases connected to your business checking account. Make arrangements with your web hosting service (the people charging you rent in order to have your website reside on their internet-connected computer) for a secure shopping cart.

People love to buy things via the computer by simply clicking a button. So if you are established with Visa® or MasterCard®, your prospect merely makes the decision to add your book to the shopping cart and, bingo, you have made a sale! Your bank account will get the money deposited into it and you will be $10-20+ dollars richer. A small charge is involved from the credit card company, but the money is yours quickly.

Of course that leaves fulfillment to you, but if someone asked for a book and you have the money in your account already, it behooves you to send the book out right away. You may also want to have separate flyers printed to accompany the book. For example, something that says, one way or another: If you like this book and want to order autographed copies for friends, just send in your check with this flyer, listing who you

*Here I am at a signing at the Ocean City, NJ library...
note the cash at the right lower corner!*

want the book sent to. Because you are a valued reader already, feel free to deduct 10% off the price for each additional book you order. We will mail the book to your friend or to you, whichever you want. (Make certain you understand state tax here.)

Offering your book via the "Net" can bring orders from around the globe, and since they are usually paying "list," further inducement can be given by saying that there will be NO SHIPPING AND HANDLING CHARGES! You cannot imagine how well that will hit your prospect's eyes!

Beyond the big scores like chain sales and little ones such as internet sales, here are those that rest in the middle.

## SELLING TO LIBRARIES

Libraries are wonderful customers, and in fact, they may turn out to be your best customer type altogether! Many will order from Baker & Taylor, Ingram, Quality, Unique, etc., but still more may want to actually buy the book from the author her/himself! So with whatever approach you take to reach these libraries, offer a gimmick too. Suggest that you will be glad to autograph the book "To The Patrons (libraries have patrons, not customers) of the XYZ Library." Tell the library that you will offer quantity discounts. You see, many libraries are part of buying groups and sometimes you don't know if a little teeny library is involved with dozens of others. I contacted one such facility in New York and wound up with orders for well over 100 books. Of course I provided a sizable discount off the cover price, but then I didn't have to mail books to 100 libraries either. The main branch sent them out to their contributing facilities!

Libraries normally pay full retail! And, of course, you know that they will pay too, without requiring you to deal with returns, or lack of income, or any other excuses. They may require more paperwork such as vouchers or purchase orders, but to sell to a library is about as good a sale as you can get, and librarians talk to each other too. If you arrange for a sale of your book, make absolutely certain you tell other libraries about it in your outreach to them. And while you are at it, if one librarian buys, ask her/him to recommend a friend or two at another facility so that you can contact them and try to sell to them as well.

Don't hesitate to cross the line from author to salesman with librarians. Of course don't "hard sell" because this will insult such people, but do let them know that you would like to get your book in front of their patrons. By the way, as noted earlier, it will help if you use that word, "patron!" A patron is a person who carries a library card and should never be referred to as a customer or client.

## MOM 'N POP STORES

Regional books sell best to local stores, but don't hesitate to try to sell your book to anyone who sells them. A variation on the chain stores too has become very popular. All the bigger operations seem to have established coffee shops right within their stores. In fact, most offer breakfast or lunch as well as a bagel and a muffin. In this way, they encourage book buyers to come, browse, pick up a book, and sit down and pour through it over a cup of tea and a Danish.

The store might wind up with some seriously messed up books that way but for sure, they have that all figured into their profit margin. While a select number of customers just come into these stores to grab a coke and sneak in some free reading or research, the majority of them do actually buy a book or two. In addition, the store makes money on the food sales as well. Traditional bookstore owners have gone this route too and you will see lots of them offering books for sale, along with food. These are good prospects for you.

So whether they sell munchies or just books, seek out the local stores and try to sell to them. Here again, as with libraries, offer personalized autographed copies as a further inducement to the owner. They can probably get the same 40% or so discount that you offer from the bigger wholesalers, but an autographed (undated) book sells better, and many will be interested in this approach. In addition, most stores have to pay shipping charges to the wholesaler so one further idea would be for you to offer "free shipping." By the way, nearly all of the smaller stores will pay outright rather than ask for consignment. Thankfully, they usually don't demand the "return" option that the wholesalers require.

You may have to wait a while to get paid, but just think, most wholesalers want you to wait for at least 90 days too!

As with library mailing lists, seek out the places that sell bookstore mailing lists. It really is important to try to find lists that are both current as well as those that contain telephone numbers. When you start this outreach, you will find that, no matter how current the list is that you buy, many, perhaps as much as 10% or more of the places that you write to or call are gone! So when you seek out bookstores as customers, realize that they work very hard for their money and regard-less, are in a tough business with failures not at all uncommon!

## SPECIALTY STORES

Here again, if your book is about a particular subject that involves specialty topics like religion, homosexuality or pornography, seek out such specific mailing lists. General lists are one way to start but if you can find one that is so specialized, don't hesitate to buy it. It can be very embarrassing to call a specialty store that has a name that cannot be identified with the subject matter of their specialty. Having called lots of stores and asked if they carry "sports books" (this is one of my approaches to getting my fishing books into stores), I can just imagine how red my face turns each time that someone on the other end says that they are a porn book store.

Remember that the grand slam home run happens quite infrequently. Although a general topic book that is not regional has a chance, a local one about your specialty is easier to sell to most stores.

## SOCIAL CLUBS

No matter how remote your area, every nook and cranny in the world has a handful of social clubs. Whether Jaycees, Exchange, Lions, etc., all of these groups of good guys exist and have meetings. Try to buy a list of them in your state or look in a few area telephone books.

Looking again in my own local area yellow pages listings, under "Clubs," I found 22 entities shown. And the book also suggests that we look up "Associations, Athletic Associations, Fraternal Organizations, Golf Courses-Public, Health Clubs; and Youth Organizations and Centers" to find still more.

Therefore, try to send out letters or at least make telephone calls to all of the clubs that might make sense as sources of book buyers. Once you are prepared to make contact, use the ideas in the following section to generate sales.

## SPECIALTY CLUBS

If your book is about their religion, religious clubs make dynamite places to contact. But don't hesitate to outreach to them about a subject of interest that is not a sensitive topic.

When you reach out to clubs, bonus buyers pop up. And you will find that the better your imagination, the more individual book sales will occur. Remember that just about every club that exists has more than just a social gathering function to serve. The majority of them are about fund raising and if you understand this you may wind up helping both yourself and the club as well.

Whatever manner of club you try to reach out to, understand that just about every one has a mailing list of members, as well as a speaker chairman. If you sincerely try to combine your sales efforts with a tie-in to helping the club, everyone will benefit.

For example, when you write your letter to the club, offer to come to meetings and speak about your subject. Don't hesitate to let the folks know that you are an expert on the topic, and that you wrote a book about it. In truth, these clubs are often hard-pressed to get members to come to meetings, and if you put something on the table that generates interest, the organization may very well be thrilled that you wrote to them.

So, if your book is about the environment, or another matter of interest to the typical "do-gooder" fraternal organization, you may be mobbed with requests to give a number of guest lectures.

## TALKS/BEING A GOOD SPEAKER

Forgive me if I dwell on this often, but selling your book can either be fun for you or living hell, depending on how you approach the subject. If you are not accustomed to public speaking, I suggest you take a course in it first because if you intend to try to sell your books this way, putting the audience to sleep won't get it done!

In a piece that he wrote for the March 2001 issue of *WD*, Richard Carlson said that you can be a good speaker if you feel good about yourself and convey self-confidence to your audience. That condenses a huge amount of instruction into one wonderful basic thought, and if you can learn from that and follow his idea, you will sell books, big time! Your listeners are there to learn about your subject matter and if you tell them just enough to keep them attentive, many will also stand in line afterwards waiting to hand you money for an autographed copy of your book!

Clubs often have funds available to pay honorariums to guest speakers. If you are very popular, you may want to restrict your attendance to meetings that will, at least, pay you a small sum for speaking. Only you can determine what makes sense for you. So, speaking fee or not plus book sales? It's up to you. Just do understand that if you do book signings at bookstores, you will probably have to hold your breath until you burst your lungs before you get a speakers fee, AND income from such sold books will go to the store instead of you. Yes, you will ultimately get your appropriate percentage out of same but talking to public gatherings away from bookstores is far more profitable.

When seeking speaking space, here's a few things you need to find out from the membership chairperson:

1. Do you pay speakers?

2. What's a normal speaker fee?

3. If travel is involved, do you pay for same, including hotel and food?

4. How many members usually attend meetings?

5. When does the meeting usually start and end, AND, at what time am I expected to give my presentation? (And am I expected to stay for the whole meeting?)

6. Will I be permitted to sell books at the meeting (before and/or after) and will a table be set up for me?

7. If smoking is a problem for you, is smoking permitted?

When you start this process, have all your ducks lined up in a row. Be very aggressive with your outreach to speaker chairmen, and offer more inducement than just giving them something of interest to give to their members.

Remember, and I use this phrase in a totally complimentary way, not as an insult, all "do-gooder" clubs have money raising as one of their main goals. So when you try to arrange for speaking tours, suggest that you will donate $____ out of the sale of each book to the club!

If your book retails at $15, then tell members that you will be glad to autograph a book to them or to a friend of theirs, and sell it at $13 instead, AND that you will be glad to pay $2 TO THEIR CLUB out of each book sold. Wow! So that book that you probably paid two bucks for and would be glad to sell a bunch at one time to stores for 40% off, or at $9 each, and maybe wait a month or two to collect, will net you $11 each instead! (And these are cash sales too!)

Time will help you with this decision, and after a while, you will know who to make such an offer to and who not — but if you are already well in the black, try this:

Regardless of the size of the function that you speak at, a two dozen or two hundred-person gathering, many listeners might like to buy a book from you but don't have cash with them. Of course if they have a checkbook, by all means, take the check. And if you are equipped already with the ability to accept credit cards, take your hardware with you so that you can run a buyer's card through it. But here's another suggestion that may be a bit startling at first ...

# JUST TRUST THEM!

If you are talking at a church or synagogue, or at a Kiwanis meeting, a condo association, or even at a gathering of any manner of specialty folks, suggest that if a member wants a copy but has no cash, check or credit card, you will trust them!

Again, pick your spot, and be in the black already, and what's the big deal if you get stiffed then?

I have been at meetings where I simply autographed a book and handed it to the surprised recipient. If you have business cards or even better, return envelopes, carry them with you. But even if you blew it and left all manner of finding you unavailable, how about the book itself? You know that your name — trade or personal, is right there in the book, with your mailing address too, somewhere within the first few pages of the front cover.

If you cannot give the recipient other means of finding where to mail payment to, the book tells them, and I bet that at least 90% of these people will send the money!

In such cases, just ask them to send the discounted price to you and forget the donation to the organization because bookkeeping will become a nightmare otherwise.

In 2001, I was selling books at a fishing flea market. I gave three books to people who didn't have enough money to pay for them right away. Within a week I got the checks from two of them but #3 never paid. Well, next year, I was at a different flea market altogether but #3 showed up at it and not only paid me what he owed me from the last year but also bought two more books that day, for cash!

Another way to "hook" a buyer who is reluctant to buy right away and is not comfortable taking the book and sending payment later would be to have sufficient handouts to give to them, so that they can order later on.

## NIGHT SCHOOL

If your subject material is regional, there is better than a 50% chance that your local high school has an adult education department that offers courses to their students in a variety of topics. You might want to attend some of these classes to assist you in fine-tuning your own writing skills. Well, those same schools may be facilities through which you can further your selling, and add more details to the resume you submit to other, bigger prospects!

Become a teacher! That's the idea, and if you persist in the attempt you may find out that several schools would like to offer a course with you as the instructor. You will be paid a modest hourly sum — maybe in the range of $15-30 an hour, plus costs. But you will also have a ready audience of book buyers too! If two dozen people sign up for your course, chances here are that the majority of them will want to buy an autographed copy from you! They may also want to pick up a few extra copies to give away as presents to friends and relatives.

Besides the teaching income and direct sales, I cannot stress sufficiently how meaningful will be the fact that your resume will now show "Instructor — in topic ABC — at XYZ School."

Make the calls, sell yourself to the person in charge of hiring instructors, and if it works, you will now be even more ready to outreach to specialty shows to give lectures.

## SPECIALTY SHOWS

Most of the bigger specialty shows pay big bucks to guest lecturers — and the range here runs from as little as $100 a speech to several thousand. (Unless you are Bill Clinton — he gets more!) You will probably also get compensated for transportation, room and board, etc. If your book is on a subject that would be of interest at specialty shows, don't hesitate to contact each and every one you can find and offer yourself as a speaker.

Forgetting the direct income, just think how many people sitting in the audience and listening to you speak will then want to buy an autographed copy of your book! This works extremely well but only if you are well prepared.

Everyone has his own approach to public speaking, and in time you will develop your own style.

The more visual aids skills you have that are of high quality, the better you should be able to hold your audience. If you will be showing slide photos though of the plants you write about in your book and the pictures are poorly taken, forget about it! Sound tape tied in with a slide presentation could be a big hitter but also could go up in a puff of smoke if you don't have something really worthwhile to show.

If you are doing visuals, you must be sure the show offers a sound and screen area for you to make a proper presentation. If you are going to do more than just talk to people, check out the facility in great detail.

If the facility is equipped for it, have a lapel microphone that allows you to walk and talk. People prefer this to having you just stand up in front of them. Work from note cards rather than scripts, or better yet, just speak to them, soliciting questions as you go along. A portable microphone is a good second choice, but it won't allow you to refer to written material as easily. Best yet would be to simply talk to them. I usually say who I am and what my subject matter is, and then tell listeners the truth: I never know what my next sentence will be so don't hesitate to interrupt me with questions — you won't be interrupting a prepared speech!

Print up a single page with your name, address, telephone and fax number on top, and on the bottom, list your book title and its cost. If you are going to charge for shipping and handling (I suggest not), say that too. And the guts of this page can be handed out to listeners to make written notes on also.

I hand out such a form that actually has ten or more specific topics listed on it, with space for notes. In this way, I have given my audience several ideas for questions in case they can't think of their own or are to shy to stick a hand up. If you are lecturing on golf at a show (or country club), have your form show, for example:

- Kind of clubs for women.
- Kind of clubs for men.
- Color vs. white golf balls.
- Public vs. private courses.

Hey, I'm not a golfer so you can probably list ten more and better topics for questions. Most important is that you will involve your listeners better this way, getting them right in the mix of things.

When you start your talk, if you are comfortable with this approach, first make sure that everyone can hear you! Introduce yourself next, and tell them about you AND your book. Don't hesitate to make reference to the book at least every five minutes — not as a direct sales approach, but just so that they will know that the book exists and can be purchased from you right after you finish talking.

Watch out for yawners or worse, sleepers. Of course if the show has been going on for hours and hours and you are the fourth speaker, the snoree could have been put away even before you began to talk.

You need to keep eye contact with everyone, so swing your head around while you speak. An involved audience translates into a full room of buyers! And again, if you do get to talk at specialty shows, that's even more experience for the impressive resume you are building to help convince still more show managers to hire you to talk! Anything you can add to a resume on your subject matter will only further enhance your selling potential. Not many professional buyers will want to buy a book from a person who doesn't have a long list of credits to talk about.

## SPECIALTY SHOW TRADE-OFFS

If you cannot convince someone to pay you to speak, ask them if they will give you selling space at a booth in exchange for giving lectures. Many show operators love this. They fill what might be otherwise empty booths and can tell prospective show attendees that there will be _____exhibitors, including you, someone who has written a book about an item of interest at the show.

Check out all the magazines that deal with your topic for ads that list such shows and contact everyone of them. If you did not produce a regional book, then outreach to everyone who has a show, everywhere. If they will not pay you to travel and put you up, this becomes a bad idea but let your judgment be your guide for which shows to try to reach.

Your computer will probably be a big help too, listing show information retrieved from the internet. Just use your imagination and you will probably think about some ways to find out about them that I haven't listed for you.

Be careful with this approach, because it could bomb out terribly. Many trade shows have speakers who also are exhibitors. If all that you can "exhibit" is your single, lonely little book, working a deal with the show manager may be a terrible suggestion. Here, only your available time and anticipation of success can trigger you to even think about this. But it does have a fine chance at being something very productive for you.

If the show runs for one day, your decision becomes easier. But if it is a two or three day event, matters such as parking, transportation, food, housing, all appear. If you are retired and single and love your subject, hey, why not try to get to all the shows you can find out about?

If you are a speaker, and have name recognition in your field, people passing your free booth may be in a fine mood to buy a handful of your books. Watch out for those who just want to talk. It's nice for your ego, but horrible for sales.

Many of them won't spring for the price of the book and also block the view of you from people who are passing by. Politely ask such people, if you have patience to listen to them, to at least stand to the side of your table so that other people can see your sign and book and what you are charging for it, etc.

# BOOK CLUBS

Your local book club is a fine source for sales, and better yet are the many nationwide clubs that have popped up within the past ten years. Some have been around for quite a while but new or old, you might sell books this way in large number. Breaking through will be the hardest job but once you have gotten their attention, significant sales can follow.

Check out *Literary Market Place* for details on how to reach out to such clubs. You can start to look for them with your own computer, of course, on the internet. A visit to your library will help as well. You may find that more effort will be involved in getting established with any clubs but it is well worth the time. As just one example of such a club, the source that I have quoted from so often, *WD,* has its own club. Call Writer's Digest Book Club in Cincinnati, Ohio to check them out. Their toll-free number is 1-800-289-0963.

Typically, a large club might pay you a fee of, say 10 to 15% of the list price, plus an amount equal to your print cost. They may even participate in the cost of printing the book! When you sell to a smaller club, you might get an amount that equals your income from selling to book wholesalers, say 40-45%, but in most such sales, the deal is complete, right then and there, with no "returns" normally involved.

Book club sales will generate income with large movement of inventory as a general rule. The bigger the sale, the lower your percentage of income but money earned sure beats having a few extra thousand copies laying around in the basement, doesn't it?

## MAILING LISTS

I have purchased mailing lists for a variety of markets. As noted, one of the best places you can outreach to is a library. While fiction books are found in libraries, unless they are real bestsellers, you will find that non-fiction books are more commonly placed on the shelves of area libraries.

In my own telephone book, under the heading "Mailing Lists," I counted six separate companies that sell mailing lists. And again, I live way out in the country. The bigger your area, the more such services you can find.

Even before you start banging your head up against the corporate structure called "Big Business," think small. Your biggest customers will be the book wholesalers who sell to the chain stores, but let's begin with libraries.

You can buy pull-off mailing labels from these firms. And depending on your budget, you can have simple or grandiose flyers printed up. The nicer the flyer, the better your chance at success, but remember, it should say something quick and brief and meaningful in order to work.

As a general rule, the mailing label provider restricts you to one single use. That means that you cannot duplicate the list and use it again and again. You actually enter into a contract with them that stipulates that you can only use the list one time. Therefore, no taking it to a fast-print facility and making copies on your own sticky tapes, okay? Chances are good to better that you will be subject to litigation. These providers often will throw in a "clinker" label, one that has the name and address of a subsidiary that is just there to test out the honesty of their customers.

You could duplicate the list and later, pull a label off and send your flyer to John Doe. Two months later may be the time to shoot out another ad to Mr. Doe. This time, you may be surprised by getting a call from someone representing the label company saying that they got a test label twice from you and that, therefore, you have broken your contract and are subject to suit. So be careful here!

# BOOK SHOWS

Book trade shows may be the very best way for you to make your book known to the largest number of potential buyers. Regional shows exist as well as ones that are national in scope. Each of these shows involves displays from the largest of publishing houses, down to the smallest. University presses are present, and many agents are in attendance. You may meet an agent who picks up a copy of your book and loves it, asking to be allowed to represent you. If that occurs, just pick yourself up off the ground, dust your pants clean, and say yes without appearing too terribly excited.

Every one of these shows offer an opportunity to people who are in the book buying field to come and rub elbows with their peers. They often seem more like social events than business, because so many are indeed friends with each other. Librarians are there, and the largest number of mom 'n pop storeowners come to such events than gather at any other function. And everyone is a potential buyer!

Contact PMA (Publishers Marketing Association) Book Exhibits in California (1-310-372-2732) to find out what shows may be available in your area when the time is right.

You may find that attendance at some of these shows will be quite costly, especially if you add in the price of a hotel room, transportation and food. But this approach could produce wonderful results for you, both for direct sales that take place right on the show floor, and for sales that will follow afterwards.

Buying space alone will not do it though. The advance brochure you get from the show will ask you if you would like to attend dinner gatherings to meet other booksellers and buyers in a more personal event. You will be asked if you would like to donate copies of your book for one manner of charitable function or another. And possibly the best way to get your book into the hands of those who buy books will be at "Signing Tables." Each show offers you the opportunity of handing autographed books to people who buy and sell them!

Now this might come as a shock at first — giving books to people instead of getting paid for them, especially since you just laid out a pile of money to get them printed! So the following is one way to give books away and have a better chance at the recipient becoming a volume buyer soon...

## PERSONAL AUTOGRAPHS!

At every book show signing that I have been at, some and often many of the people standing in line ask you to simply date and sign the book. Watch out for this one, please! 99% of the people who ask for a signed and dated book without a reference to the name of the recipient are just looking to stock their shelves with free inventory. This may sound cold on my part, but trust me, I am right more often than not about this. So how do you handle such a person without insulting them?

Pre-sign and date a small supply of books before you get into the signing chair. When a person asks for a book, ask for their name so that you can personally sign the book to them! Or ask if they are giving it to a friend or relative as a present, and get the ultimate recipient's name to write in. If the person in front of you persists in saying that they just want an auto-graphed book, count on the purpose being what I said above — they want free stuff so that they can make a sale without having had to pay for the book in the first place.

When you do autograph a book to a specific person, make sure you spell the name correctly. You don't want to give a book to Brian when he is Bryan or Kathy if she is Cathy!

Book signings at shows can be great sales inducers!

## "BOOK FAIRS"

On the other hand, you may hear about an event that is called a "book fair" and if you have in mind making a big score at these events, make sure you know what the concept is first.

You see, more often than not a "book fair" is held at an open air forum, maybe in a school yard or behind a library, and just about all of them won't work for you at all! You see, the majority deal with the sale of USED BOOKS (also known as CHEAP books).

So if you are standing out there with your wonderful brandy new book that cost you $2 a copy and expect to sell a box full within the first hour because the street is filled with folks milling around, forget it! You will not be able to sell the book at retail, and not even at wholesale, because most of these browsers are bargain hunters, looking to spend a buck or two at most. Book fairs that are indoors and do not involve the sale of used books could work out just fine, but don't jump to go to one without first understanding just exactly what the premise of the event really is.

## WHEN TO/TELEMARKETING

"800" numbers offer a great temptation, but when selling, try to avoid dialing one if you also have a regular number to dial. While some places that offer 800 numbers might not care, you still will be in a better position to achieve success if you pay for your calls. This applies if you are thinking about calling a university press *(see Chapter Seven)*, or anyone else you are outreaching to. Even if someone were offering you the bargain of your life, you still would rather that they pay for the call, right? Please keep that in mind when you are trying to make a sale via the telephone. I had an 800 number for my insurance agency and really found it quite offensive when someone called me on it to try and sell me anything!

Telemarketing can be a separate book, actually. While we all cringe when we quickly recognize a caller who is really trying to sell us something, you yourself can generate a superb amount of sales on the telephone. What you must do is learn from your own personal concerns. For example, you know that you hate to get a telemarketer's call during dinner. And for sure, if you are a late sleeper, you certainly don't want someone waking you up at 8:30 a.m. who wants to sell you a subscription to a newspaper. If you are religious and observe Saturday or Sunday, how do you feel when someone calls you on your Sabbath who really hopes you will buy his storm windows?

The bottom line is that you must put yourself into the shoes of the person who you are calling and try to think like they think.

If you want to sell your book to a mom 'n pop store, never, not ever, call them on a Saturday, period! That is their busiest day by far and you will be insulting them by trying to peddle your book while they have a store full. On the other hand, if the store is empty on a Saturday, they cannot afford to even stay open for business, not the least being their desire to buy yet more stock. Moreover, if the store also has a dining area, don't call them around lunch for gosh sakes! This also applies to libraries. Never call them on a Thursday evening or a Saturday. They are far too busy to concentrate on your words.

To properly sell your book over the telephone requires you to handle the prospective buyer in the same manner as you would like to be treated. Don't waste their time or yours. A sales approach that has helped me substantially with bookstore deals involves a few quick and simple questions. For example, "Do you sell new books?" (If they are a used bookstore, they probably won't buy your book!) Next, "Do you sell books about _____ ?" (The blank involves your subject matter.) The store may be a children's bookstore, maybe an "adult book" store, or a religious bookstore, and if you can quickly weed out the kinds of stores that you know won't carry the kind of book you wrote, you will eliminate lots of extra work.

If you ask them if they sell books about, for example, golf, they may think that you want to BUY such a book. But if their answer is yes, quickly tell them that you don't want to buy a book but instead want to sell them your book about golf.

Make certain early on that you find out if you have a decision-maker on the phone. In bookstores, ask for the owner or manager after you find out if they sell the kind of book that you wrote. Do this too with libraries. Try to get the reference librarian or head librarian.

For openers, make sure that you have negotiated the best telephone rates possible. Just think, postage for each first class form letter that you shotgun out to a zillion prospective stores costs over 40 cents each, including the cost of the form letter and envelope. On the other hand, you may get telephone rates that make the cost per minute as little as a nickel or a dime.

When you start the process, until you get a good handle on it, get one of those little egg timers. Buy one that runs out of sand in a minute or at worst, two minutes. If your phone rate is 7 cents and you can contain calls to less than two minutes, you only spent a third of what your form letter cost you! And your response to telephone call sales attempts will be far more successful than your letter will be, count on it. That doesn't mean that you should avoid letter writing, but do realize that folks who concentrate on such selling attempts are usually happy if they get 5% response. If you telemarket carefully with the right approach, you might find that as many as $\frac{1}{3}$ of the store owners you call will actually buy from you — or will at least buy from a wholesaler who you sell to!

Traditionally, all things being equal, sale success percentage works, in order, this way — #1, by far, from in-person visits. #2, telephone calls. #3, full price postage mail offerings. #4, — way, way down — bulk mail offerings.

If you are retired, you have a leg up on the people who still work for a living. You see, making calls requires a lot of excess time on weekdays! So if you cannot do this at such times, you will either have to take a day or two off every now and then to concentrate on telephone sales attempts, or go with a different approach.

One different approach was referred to many pages back in the "Partnership" section. What if your partner is retired? Give her/him the job of selling! And what if your tongue gets so tied when you try to hustle sales that you feel that you are going to wet your pants from fright? Again, a partner may be the answer. You can also add that you may have a poor telephone personality, or you may have a heavy accent, or who knows how many other reasons that you are dead certain will kill you in telemarketing. Well, back to "Partnership," dear reader, for a solution!

Making telephone calls to chain stores may even accelerate sales. Use the same basic approach. Never call on a Saturday or a Thursday evening or at lunchtime since they are too busy then. Ask if they carry the kind of book that you wrote about or maybe you can even ask them if they carry the actual book itself! If you have sold a supply to the bigger wholesalers, the chain may actually carry your book. And if not, you are telling them about it that way.

Do try to get someone in management though because trying to get a clerk to buy your book will be suicide. While decisions to carry books in the chains are nearly always made at the home office level, quite a few stores are allowed to make "Manager Buys." You have an even better chance at getting a manager to buy if your book is regional in scope, or perhaps timely — such as if it is about Christmas and your calendar reads November lst.

What is critically important is to get good telephone lists. These can be purchased in the same manner as mailing lists can be obtained. Or for that matter, the wonderful world of the internet gives you substantial access.

When calling, whether libraries, stores, etc., be strong, not weak, and forceful, rather than pushy. Don't try to sell over the telephone if you are frightened at the mere thought of it. But do know that the wild rush you will get when the voice at the other end of the phone asks you to tell them about your book will be immeasurable. As the questions proceed and you move towards a "sale," your little heart will pound, big time. Getting a storeowner to say "Send me a half-dozen," could be a fireworks display for you. Just make sure you get the correct spelling of the buyer's name as well as the mailing address of where to send the books plus a separate address for billing, if it exists. Seek a purchase order number, too, if that is part of the system they use.

Telemarketing can be your most fun, and if you develop a positive approach, it will probably be the thing that sells more books for you than anything else. Just keep good, accurate records — maybe by alphabetical order, listing what calls you made and what the results. If you were asked to call back (leave a message if you want but you will normally not get return calls), do so when you were asked to call. Try to send faxes too, which tell the buyer about your book. And then follow it up afterwards.

One of the worst mistakes that a bookseller can make (the same error that nearly all salespeople make) involves following up for subsequent sales. The best buyer is a store that bought your book and sold out! But hardly any of them will ever call and order more! Yes, if they bought a dozen three months ago and still have all of them left, maybe that store isn't the best to try to sell more to. But if they are sold out or only have one or two copies left, you know that you have a satisfied store on your hands and selling more stock to them will be like duck soup!

## MAINTAIN YOUR OWN LIST

Start with the basic premise that no one cares as much about the sale of your book as you do and work out from there. That being the case, a list of your books, by computer and in print, with a calendar for assistance, can help you with selling. Going back once more to *WD*, in the January 2000 edition, Jeffery D. Zbar illustrates how you can cover all bases in "marketing, branding, and writing success." This one single piece may very well be the best guide you can get towards how to sell. I urge you to try and get a back copy of the magazine.

Among his thoughts within this article were ways to get an editor or client to buy from you. Well, let's expand on that now. Creating a list of buyers or prospective buyers is critical to your success.

Put a list together of each and every store or librarian that buys from you. Enter the name of the facility, its address, telephone and fax number, as well as the name of the person who kicked out the order to you. And then put a separate list together of those who said maybe. Prepare these lists in alphabetical order. You may want to put a few together, one for libraries and another for retail stores. If you have been in contact with wholesalers, have a separate grouping set aside for them as well with full details.

Leave room in each listing for your own comments, with space to write in notes from each subsequent follow up letter or call you make. If you cannot find the person you seek, try to send a fax to them instead. Work with a calendar also, to help insure that you will actively continue to seek sales.

Remember that anyone who has bought from you is a potential subsequent buyer as well. No matter how good the records are in retail bookstores, rarely, if ever, will anyone know to place a re-order with you once they are either sold out or only have one copy left. Again, if they bought from you already, call those stores even more often for renewal sales.

Writing a book, self-publishing it, and then selling it, can be among the most wonderful experiences you can ever be involved with. I hope that you have learned enough from this book to give you the ability to sit yourself down at your computer and get started.

Just remember, check out Dan Poynter's book, "The Self-Publishing Manual," as well as buy a subscription to *WD* to keep up to date. You can order your subscription by calling 1-800-333-0133.

# CHAPTER NINE

# Electronic
# Book Publishing

By the time you write your book, you may find that your audience prefers to read your work of art on a computer screen. Therefore, be ready for that group early. Steve Outing and Amy Gahran wrote a fine piece in the January 2000 issue of *WD*. They offer the idea that your book need not be in paper form alone to be a winner in the 21st century. In a subsequent article that Mr. Outing wrote for *WD* in March of 2001, he told readers still more about the wonders of digital reading.

As an author, when you are setting the price of your book, you must take into consideration the costs of professional help in cover design, typesetting, and printing as well as physical inventory space and potential damage. However, another possibility exists which would allow you to offer the book at a lower price!

If you are quite computer literate and feel that your target audience is also, then another option is electronic book publishing.

Now, books can be delivered electronically. Information can be delivered faster and cheaper by downloading from the internet. Authors can spend more time writing and less time managing production and delivery. Customers can find information quickly and at less cost.

Let's say you decide you will not go through the traditional printing of your book, but rather will market it as an e-book.

How does this work?

Just as you would plan to market in traditional ways over the internet (from your website and other sites such as Amazon.com), you can also market using specialty sites. So your e-book will be found on:

- Your website if you have one
- Amazon.com, BarnesandNoble.com, etc.
- Sites that specialize in e-books
- Links on other internet sites that you have arranged for

Your book will come to the attention of the prospective buyer because there is a cover shot and intriguing description. Cover shot? Yes, even e-books need to have a graphic representation of the cover of the book, so you will need artwork to simulate a book cover. Add reviews and an author biography to build credibility.

To pique the customer's interest, the site may offer to e-mail the first chapter for free.

The customer will add the book to a shopping cart and pay with a credit card, just as they would for a hardcopy book. Then they download the book to their personal computer and will have a certain amount of time, usually 30-60 days, to read it with an e-book reader.

## WHAT IS AN E-BOOK READER?

To back up for a moment, the book is going to be downloaded to the customer's personal computer in a particular way. It will probably be a "PDF" (Portable Document Format) file, which is an industry standard. The program that reads this PDF file is called Adobe Acrobat®.

Before downloading the PDF, the Adobe Acrobat software must be on the PC. This software is free and can either be downloaded from the e-book website or from the Adobe website. Just go to www.adobe.com and click "Download Acrobat Reader." (There are other "readers," such as the Microsoft Reader®, but Adobe Acrobat is the most popular.)

When the book is downloaded, it will have some encryption that protects the publisher's copyrights and determines how long the customer has to read it. Most publishers restrict the printing and disable the e-book reader's print function; however, if it is your decision not to, your book can be printed.

For all but the largest books, it should take less than 2 minutes of connection time to transfer the book to the PC.

To see how e-books are handled on Amazon.com, go to their site (www.amazon.com) and search on e-books. The FAQ's (Frequently Asked Questions) are very helpful. The main difference between Amazon and other e-book sites is that once the purchase is complete, Amazon will send the customer an e-mail message, which contains a link to a webpage where the download can be initiated.

Websites that contain helpful information on e-books are:

- www.booklocker.com
- www.overdrive.com

You may be thinking about increasing sales by developing your own website.

To gain an understanding of how to accomplish this, check out the next chapter "Creating Your Own Website." Unless you really are an expert, I suggest you contact a website designer and sit down and put your own site together. This could increase your sales immeasurably. When you get into book #2 and then #3, you will certainly have the opportunity of displaying all your books to increase overall sales potential.

Here are a few experts who can help you:

■ Karen Kelly who owns Dialog Solutions, Inc., in Alexandria Township, NJ. Reach her at 1-908-996-2145 or by fax, 1-908-996-7421. (Karen designed my website, wrote the next chapter in this book, and is also my wife!) My site is www.gonefishinbooks.com.

■ Prometheon.com is in Santa Barbara, CA. Call Michael Frick there at 1-805-563-7731. His fax # is 1-805-563-3391.

CHAPTER TEN

# Creating Your Own Website

*By Karen Kelly*

Many books have been written on the subject of creating a website. This chapter will provide an overview of the necessary steps and introduce the terminology frequently used, so that by the end of the chapter you will have some background and ideas on how to proceed. Hopefully the terminology and concepts will not be too daunting so you can hold your own as you work with the experts.

There are 5 central questions to ask:

1. **What will be the name of my website?**
2. **What should my website look like?**
3. **Will I accept credit card orders on my website?**
4. **How do I get my site on the internet?**
5. **How will people find my site?**

## 1. WHAT WILL BE THE NAME OF MY WEBSITE?

There are 2 parts to naming your website.

The first is to invent a name that describes your business, is easy to type and easy to remember.

The second is to find out if the name is already in use and reserve it.

When you invent the name that describes your business, it will be in 3 parts:

- www.
- your name goes here
- .com

Although there are suffixes other than ".com", most businesses use it and most people expect the website to end in it. (There are other specialized endings such as .org, .edu, .gov, .net, and .biz but they require a visitor to pause and make the mental adjustment to get the site address correct and are therefore less desirable.)

Due to popularity, there are almost no single word names available any more and most phrases are taken. Make up your own phrase or combination and try for brevity. Also, capitals don't matter when typing in a website address, so use them for clarity in advertising your site.

For example, when Manny was looking to name his website, the process was:

- Fishin — *taken*
- Fishing — *taken*
- GoneFishing — *taken*
- GoneFishin — *taken*
- Manny — *taken*
- GoneFishinBooks — *open*
- GoneFishingBooks — *open*

How do you know if the name is already in use? It is not sufficient to just type in the website address into your browser and see if something comes up.

Website addresses are purchased and reserved in the name of the purchaser. In this context, a website address is called a Domain Name. Even though you type in the Domain Name you desire and a "Page Not Found" error is displayed, it does not mean that the name is available.

In order to find out if the name is available, play around with these websites:

■ www.easywhois.com
■ www.networksolutions.com

Type in the name you want, and any registration information will be shown. If your desired name is taken, you always have the option of contacting the purchaser to see if they will let you buy it from them and re-register it. Note also that names are reserved and paid up for a certain number of years, and the name you want may be coming up for expiration.

If your desired domain name is reserved but not actually being used as a website yet, and you really really want it, you have 3 choices:

1. Contact the owner and buy it.
2. Use .biz instead of .com, which is a nice new domain name extension.
3. If you see that the name is up for renewal soon, Network Solutions site has an option for you to backorder your name at a cost of $69, and they will continually search for its availability for a year. If the owner fails to renew, they will grab it for you.

There may be special circumstances where you want to reserve two names but have either one point to the same location. For example the word "fishin" in the website, www.GoneFishinBooks.com is so similar to the word "fishing" that it is easy to see how prospects could type in another site name, www.GoneFishingBooks.com.

For that reason, both names are reserved and paid for and automatic redirection is in place. Transparently, this redirects any visitors who type "fishing" to the correct website address. Upon request, the web hosting service sets up the redirection.

Finally, once you have determined that the Domain Name is available, how do you reserve and pay for it?

There are two ways. The first is to go directly to a Domain Name registration service. The second way, which can be less expensive and easier, is to go through your web hosting service.

If you are not yet ready to establish a relationship with a web hosting service but want to ensure that the name you want is reserved, then search on Yahoo® or AOL® or your favorite search engine and contact a Domain Name registration service such as www.lowestdomainrates.com (which I am not necessarily recommending... just giving you a place to start).

Be forewarned that the registration process will generate a lot of junk email! And like magazine subscriptions, they will try to get you to renew even though you have a year left.

When you are ready to go ahead with a web hosting service, tell them that you already have a domain name reserved. They will probably ask you to contact the organization you dealt with and have ownership of the name transferred to them. They call this "taking over the name." Here's where the cheaper and easier part comes in — had you been ready, you would not have to transfer the name (potential breakdown here) and the web hosting service probably would have thrown in the domain name registration either free or for a much smaller fee.

## 2. WHAT SHOULD MY WEBSITE LOOK LIKE?

If you have a substantial budget, then there are many services available to design a website. Simply go to www.yahoo.com or your favorite search engine and search on "website design" to get started.

If you prefer to be more involved, and even do the design yourself, then this chapter will help you understand designing your website and getting it to the internet.

When you begin to think about what your website should look like, the best way to start is to look at other websites and decide what design elements you like. For most websites, understated is better. Garish colors, blinking objects, busy background wallpaper all make it difficult for the reader to stay on the page and read your message. Let's assume for the moment that you are drawing your website on paper.

The basic web page usually is what is called a 3-pane interface.

| Frame #1 |
|---|
| BANNER goes here -- your company name and logo. |
| (Sometimes this area is smaller on pages other than the Home Page.) |

| Frame #2 | Frame #3 |
|---|---|
| Menu options go here. | "Content" goes here – when a menu option is clicked, the results show up here.<br><br><br><br><br>********<br>Company Name<br>Company Address<br>Company Phone #<br>Company Fax #<br>Company E-mail Address<br><br>Disclaimers & Copyrights<br>(Sometimes this is in a 4$^{th}$ frame and does not scroll off the page.) |

Up until now, we have assumed that you are designing your website on paper. Now let's talk about tools you'll need to go further.

■ **Web Page Designer Software.** There exists commercial software in all price ranges to support the novice web designer. The one that seems to be the most robust and popular for the least cost is Microsoft Front Page®. There are even classes in high school Adult Education and community college night school taught by computer professionals for a reasonable cost; however, web page design can be learned quickly at home.

The software will allow you to create a blank page (the

Home Page) and you can begin to place frames (lines to form boxes) according to the Frame 1, 2, 3 etc. model above. Then you may assign a background color to the page or frame. Add text after selecting the style, font and point size. Add logos and pictures *(see Color Scanner below)*.

If you are following the 3-pane model above, create the menu options panel.

Once you have the Home Page created, the rest of the pages in the site can be created. When all the pages are complete, use a menu option in the web page design software to create hotlinks from the menu options and choose which page to link to.

To help with navigation, it is recommended to have a Home option and possibly Previous (Back) to navigate back to the prior page. In addition, if you have a large site or one with a catalog, a Search option is desirable. Another popular navigation tool is called "breadcrumbs", which appears on the page as a sequence of pages visited, e.g.:

Home <— Front Cover <— Back Cover

This communicates that the prospect began at the Home page, looked at the page showing the Front Cover and book description, and now is looking at the page with the Back Cover. Any page title shown in the list is "hot" and will navigate immediately to that page. To actually see this in operation, visit www.gonefishinbooks.com.

■ **Color Scanner.** If you have a company logo or pictures to include in the site, you will need to purchase a color scanner of medium-range quality and scan the items into your computer as files. The scanner can also be used to scan your book covers, front and back and the Table of Contents if you like.

Then you define an area of your web page as a picture, and choose the file name from a list of all the picture files in your computer. Once you choose the file name, the picture or graphic will display in that area of the page.

## 3. WILL I ACCEPT CREDIT CARD ORDERS ON MY WEBSITE?

The most important decision to make is whether to conduct what is called "e-commerce." Will you accept orders using a credit card? Or will you direct customers to send you their order and a check through the mail?

If you choose to accept credit cards, the site will be more complex due to the security that must be provided, much if not all of which your "web hosting service" will handle (see next section). We've all heard horror stories where hackers broke into websites and stole credit card information. It is crucial that you assure customers that their information is safe by having, for example, a logo on that web page from a company like Verisign. The other indication of a secure shopping cart page is a little gold lock on the bottom right portion of the screen.

By the way, in case you're thinking like so many others that your site will just format the credit card information into an email and send it to you, let me assure you that email is very far from secure. Think about it for a moment... it is bouncing from computer to computer around the world and is subject to programs called "sniffers" (not to mention the computer administrators, the human "sniffers") that specialize in capturing valuable information.

## 4. HOW DO I GET MY SITE ON THE INTERNET?

To be available for viewing on the worldwide web (a.k.a. internet), the coding for your website must reside on a computer (also called a "file server," or "server" for short) that is connected to the internet. As an aside because you may hear this term, the computer code is called "HTML" which is automatically generated from your software (such as Front Page).

As you are going through this process, there will be people who tell you that you can save money by just using your own computer as your file server and connect it to the internet.

Unless you are a writer who is also a computer professional, please don't attempt this. Remember, hackers are always looking to break into computers. You run more than the normal risk of viruses and general mayhem, as well as the infamous Denial of Service attacks that overwhelm a computer with a tremendous volume of requests and take down the website completely. Additionally, a very successful computer professional I know with his own international consulting firm had his website taken over by a Chinese pornography company. He watched for days as they tried to break in to his file server, and they eventually did.

And do you really want to have a computer running 24 hours a day, 7 days a week in your guest bedroom or garage?

A "web hosting service" will, for a fee, allow you to transfer your web pages to their file server connected to the internet.

As always, word of mouth is best in finding a good web hosting service. They all will promise to have your website up "24 by 7" (a.k.a. 24/7), which means 24 hours a day, 7 days a week. But what are their reliability statistics? When you ask them, they should be over 99%.

However, the key to having a good web hosting service is their responsiveness. How long does it take for you to have your questions answered? Even more importantly, how long does it take for them to fix problems? Do they make you go through layers of bureaucracy and then give you unresponsive answers?

When I first contracted with my web hosting service, they would accept phone calls and provide technical support on the spot. At one point, the website functioned perfectly. Then certain features broke and the usage statistics stopped working. They stopped taking calls and stopped responding to email. They put web pages up on their site which the customer had to fill out to report problems. Sometimes they respond to problems, sometimes they ignore them. Sometimes they blame the problems on other organizations when it's really their fault. When you've paid for a year and are left twisting in the wind, it's no fun.

Hopefully, someone you know is happy with their provider and can give you a recommendation. If not, search on Yahoo or whatever search engine you prefer for "web hosting service" and see if you can assess their level of responsiveness after speaking with them.

To transfer your website from Front Page or whatever development product you used to the hosting service, use an "FTP" program (File Transfer Protocol). There are many out there that are free, and some will allow 30 days of usage before a one-time payment must be made of around $40. Ask your web hosting service which they prefer or use "Cute FTP," which comes with a free trial, at www.cuteftp.com.

The web hosting service will give you three pieces of information so that you can do the transfer to their server — the password for the server, its IP address (a number like 100.200.300.01) and the file directory they want you to use.

## 5. HOW WILL PEOPLE FIND MY SITE?

Other than you going around publicizing the name of your website, it is critical that the site name must be found and listed in the results of an online search.

There are many "search engines" on the internet. Your site must be found when search terms (called "keywords") are typed into the Search box in order for you to generate traffic to your site.

Part of this job belongs to you, and part to the web hosting service.

What you need to do is develop a list of keywords that should cause your site to be listed as a hit. So for this book, a preliminary list might be:

- Luftglass
- Publishing
- Self-publishing
- Writing

Always include your last name so that the search results can show everywhere your name appears on the internet. If you have arranged for a site such as Amazon.com to sell your book, this will even cause a hit on the Amazon.com web page with your book on it!

Once you give the list to the web hosting service, they will make the arrangements for your site to be listed on the most famous search engines — Yahoo!, Google, AOL, Lycos®, Excite®, and AltaVista®. Unfortunately, the time has passed when listings were free. And you may have wondered why certain websites are first on the hits list... they, of course, paid extra!

Having your website found by the AOL search engine is a special case and requires technical expertise beyond that needed for the other engines. Your web hosting service must get your site listed and continually verify that your presence is still shown to people interested in your products and services on all the engines. There may be a separate charge for this, in the neighborhood of $150 a month. To get your site always listed at the top can cost much more.

Lastly, your web hosting provider should capture statistics so that you can see if your site is being visited. Usually they will attach an extra page to your website to display the statistics, and give you the exact address ("URL") to type in. If you want a counter on the Home Page that displays the number of visitors to your site so far, your web design software will have an option for this. However, just so you know, you will have to coordinate this with your web hosting service because they have to have their piece set up and running on their server already.

*Got all that? Now go out and write your own book!*
*I hope you get writer's cramp signing all the ones you sell!*

*'Scuze me, gone fishin'.*

PLEASE FILL IN AS MUCH INFORMATION AS POSSIBLE OR APPLICABLE *RETURN ENTIRE FORM* TO:

# ADVANCE BOOK INFORMATION
R.R. BOWKER DATA COLLECTION CENTER
P.O. BOX 6000, OLDSMAR, FL 34677-6800

TITLE: _____

SUBTITLE: _____

Title Volume Number: _____

PUBLISHER (Not Printer): _____

ADDRESS: _____

Is this a set? Yes☐ No☐ **Number of Volumes:** _____

Pub. Date: (MM/YY) _____ / _____

PHONE: _____ TOLL FREE: _____

FAX: _____ E-mail: _____

Web site: _____

Copyright Date: (year) _____

Pages: _____ Illustrated?: ☐ YES ☐ NO

Status: ☐ Active ☐ On Demand ☐ Out-of-Print

IMPRINT (If other than company name): _____

DISTRIBUTOR (if other than publisher): _____
(If you distribute foreign books, please send us a copy of your documentation and indicate whether distribution is exclusive or non-exclusive. Currently, only exclusive distributors are included in the US portion of the BIP database.)

**CONTRIBUTOR NAME (A=Author, E=Editor, I=Illustrator, P=Photographer, T=Translator):**

Contributor _____ ☐A ☐E ☐I ☐P ☐T ☐Other_____
(check all that apply)

Contributor _____ ☐A ☐E ☐I ☐P ☐T ☐Other_____
(check all that apply)

Contributor _____ ☐A ☐E ☐I ☐P ☐T ☐Other_____
(check all that apply)

Series Title: _____

Series Subtitle: _____ Series Volume Number: _____

Edition Info.: ☐Reprint ☐ Revised ☐ Abridged ☐Large Type ☐ Unabridged ☐ Deluxe ☐ Other(specify)_____ Edition No. ____

E-Book File Format: ☐ASCII Text ☐ HTML ☐ MS Word ☐ PDF ☐ RTF ☐ Other(specify)_____

E-Book Edition Info.: ☐ Rocket ☐ SoftBook ☐ PalmPilot ☐ Millennium ☐ EveryBook ☐ Other(specify) _____

Audience: (children's books require grade levels) GRADES: _____ AGES: _____
☐Juvenile ☐Young Adult ☐College ☐Other (specify) _____

Original Title: (if previously published & changed) _____

Translated Title: _____

Current Language (if other than English): _____ Original Language (if translated): _____

Publisher Order No.: _____ LCControl No.(LCCN): _____

Point Size (LARGE TYPE BKS): _____ Book Size: _____ Book Weight: _____

For ISBN Applicants: Fill out this form for each of your titles and return with your application. When your copy is returned to you with your ISBN log book, assign an ISBN to each title, enter it below, and return the form(s) to the R.R. Bowker Data Collection Center, Oldsmar, Florida. This will allow your title(s) to be listed in Books In Print or complete the ABI form online at www.bowker.com/titleforms/home/index.html.
ISBN Note: Write full 10-digit number in space below. The BIP system requires a separate ISBN for each edition and binding.

| BINDING | ISBN | PRICE | *TYPE: | **CURRENCY | MARKET | |
|---|---|---|---|---|---|---|
| Hardcover: ☐ Trade ☐Textbk | _____ | $___.___ | _____ | _____ | US_____ | CAN_____ |
| Paperback: ☐ Trade ☐Textbk | _____ | $___.___ | _____ | _____ | US_____ | CAN_____ |
| ☐Library Binding | _____ | $___.___ | _____ | _____ | US_____ | CAN_____ |
| ☐Mass Market | _____ | $___.___ | _____ | _____ | US_____ | CAN_____ |
| ☐E-Book | _____ | $___.___ | _____ | _____ | US_____ | CAN_____ |
| ☐Other:_____ | _____ | $___.___ | _____ | _____ | US_____ | CAN_____ |

*Price type refers to invoice, retail, tentative, etc.
**Currency refers to US, Canadian, etc.

Type of Work: ☐ Non-Fiction ☐ Fiction ☐ Poetry ☐ Drama ☐ Essay ☐ Other _____

Subject Area: ☐ Children's (CB) ☐ Law(LB) ☐ Med(MB) ☐ Relig(RB) ☐ Sci-Tech(ST) ☐ Other _____

**OVER PLEASE→**

Description of Content: _____

_____
_____
_____
_____
_____
_____
_____
_____
_____

# BISG MAJOR SUBJECTS

The Book Industry Study Group (BISG) has developed a list of **2800** subjects and subject codes. Known as the BISAC Subject Heading List, they are used to describe the subject contents of a book. Below you will find a list of **48 major BISAC categories.** If you are interested in using the full BISAC subject Headings List, you may write to BISG at 160 Fifth Ave., New York, NY 10010, or call 212-929-1393, or e-mail bill@bookinfo.org.

**Please be advised that even if you use these headings, you should still complete the section above entitled "Description of Content"** so that your book can be properly classified.

## Please Indicate Appropriate Subject(s)

❑ANTIQUES & COLLECTIBLES
❑ARCHITECTURE
❑ART
❑BIOGRAPHY & AUTOBIOGRAPHY
❑BODY, MIND & SPIRIT (formerly OCCULTISM / PARAPSYCHOLOGY)
❑BUSINESS & ECONOMICS
❑COMPUTERS
❑COOKING
❑CRAFTS & HOBBIES
❑CURRENT EVENTS
❑DRAMA
❑EDUCATION
❑FAMILY & RELATIONSHIPS
❑FICTION
❑FOREIGN LANGUAGE STUDY
❑GAMES
❑GARDENING
❑HEALTH & FITNESS
❑HISTORY
❑HOUSE & HOME
❑HUMOR
❑JUVENILE FICTION
❑JUVENILE NONFICTION
❑LANGUAGE ARTS & DISCIPLINES

❑LAW
❑LITERARY CRITICISM & COLLECTIONS
❑MATHEMATICS
❑MEDICAL
❑MUSIC
❑NATURE
❑PERFORMING ARTS
❑PETS
❑PHILOSOPHY
❑PHOTOGRAPHY
❑POETRY
❑POLITICAL SCIENCE
❑PSYCHOLOGY & PSYCHIATRY
❑REFERENCE
❑RELIGION
❑SCIENCE
❑SELF-HELP
❑SOCIAL SCIENCE
❑SPORTS & RECREATION
❑STUDY AIDS
❑TECHNOLOGY
❑TRANSPORTATION
❑TRAVEL
❑TRUE CRIME

# Index

# Order Form

For additional copies of this book, or any of the ten *Gone Fishin'* series *(see back cover)*, please send check or money order to:

**Gone Fishin' Enterprises**
PO Box 556
Annandale, NJ 08801

- New Jersey residents please add 6% state sales tax.
- Tell me who you'd like the book autographed to.
- There will no shipping or handling charges.

For bulk orders call: 908 996-2145

Look up *Gone Fishin'* books at:
**www.gonefishinbooks.com**

----------------------------------------------------------------

Name:_____

Address:_____

City: _____ State: _____ Zip:_____

Autograph To: _____

*Please send me:*

| # of Copies | Book Title | Price |
|---|---|---|
| _____ | **So You Want To Write A Book** ................$13.95 | |
| _____ | Gone Fishin'... In Spruce Run Reservoir ............$12.95 | |
| _____ | Gone Fishin'... In Round Valley Reservoir ...........$13.95 | |
| _____ | Gone Fishin'... In N.J. Saltwater Rivers And Bays ......$14.95 | |
| _____ | Gone Fishin'... For Carp ........................$12.95 | |
| _____ | Gone Fishin'... With Kids ........................$ 9.95 | |
| _____ | Gone Fishin'... The 100 Best Spots In New Jersey .....$16.00 | |
| _____ | Gone Fishin'... In Lake Hopatcong ................$13.95 | |
| _____ | Gone Fishin'... The 100 Best Spots In New York ......$16.00 | |
| _____ | Gone Fishin'... The 50 Best Waters In Pennsylvania ....$13.95 | |
| _____ | Gone Fishin'... The 75 Best Waters In Connecticut ....$13.95 | |